Richard Burton

Bishop Burton
COLLEGE

Sports Coaching
and Teaching
Tony Gummerson

A & C Black · London

First published 1992 by
A & C Black (Publishers) Ltd
35 Bedford Row, London WC1R 4JH

© 1992 Tony Gummerson

ISBN 0 7136 3575 4

A CIP catalogue record for this book is available from
the British Library.

Photoset in Linotron Palatino by
Rowland Phototypesetting Ltd,
Bury St Edmunds, Suffolk
Printed and bound in Great Britain by
The Bath Press, Avon

Contents

— • —

CONTENTS

Acknowledgements

The production of this book was made possible by the help and encouragement of several coaches committed to the development of coach education.

John Horan has applied his analytical mind to many of my theoretical implications of coaching theory and has made them work. He has also managed to push back the frontiers of applied sports medicine and good practice in coaching.

David Hodgson has given me the opportunity to apply some of my ideas in a sporting context. He has always provided me with support when the going was difficult.

Carl Johnson has done more than any person I know to raise the status and credibility of coaches, primarily those in athletics but also by association in other sports as well.

Wilf Paish, my own coach and lifelong friend, has nurtured my interest in coaching by his own exemplary activities in athletics. Wilf has chartered the development of Olympic, World and National champions in athletics and several other sports.

Ian Read, artist and coach, has guided me through my coaching activities. His aesthetic appreciation of coaching as an art has been a constant source of inspiration. His understanding of the function of the coach in the overall development of the individual is a model for all coaches and educators.

Thanks are also due to Brian Aldred for the cartoons in this book and to Taurus Graphics for the line drawings.

What's in a name?
— • —

The trend in sport and recreation is to use the word 'coach' when referring to the person who imparts his knowledge to those who wish to learn and benefit from his expertise. However, in most physical activities and sports the term 'coach' is used along with 'instructor', 'teacher', 'trainer', 'adviser' and 'consultant', together with a whole range of terms of respect and authority. Throughout this book the word 'coach' is used predominantly. Where 'instructor', 'teacher' and 'trainer' are included they have the same meaning as 'coach', unless otherwise specified.

Coaches, students, participants and athletes are, in the main, referred to individually as 'he'. This of course should be taken to mean 'he or she' where appropriate.

Introduction

— • —

There is no doubt that sport, exercise, recreation and physical activity in general play a major part in modern life styles. It might be said that the desire to learn, play and enjoy a sport is one of the most fundamental of human needs. It can offer many years of enjoyment, well being, social relationships and self-development. Participants range from committed, dedicated sportsmen and women who wish to compete at the highest possible national and international levels to those who enjoy the less physically demanding but equally important social, recreative and fun elements. For some there are considerable financial benefits to be gained from success, while for others the reward is simply an increase in fitness, and better general health. The reasons why individuals participate in physical activity are as varied as the opportunities available. Participation in sport and recreation has become a very important area of research for sociologists, psychologists and economists alike!

The increase in numbers of participants has placed great demands not only on facility providers but also on those organisations and individuals who promote specific activities and provide the necessary technical back up and support. There is no doubt that sport and recreation have become 'big business', and for the media they offer an unlimited source of material.

Though some sports remain truly amateur, participation being only for pure enjoyment and the associated social benefits, there are now many opportunities for money to be made. The rewards of success can be great and many individuals seek a professional career in a variety of sporting activities.

With the enhanced status of sport and recreation in society the provision of instruction has become very important, although the need for competent coaches has long been recognised. Over 3,000 years ago the Greeks saw the need to provide effective and efficient coaching for the competitors taking part in the Olympic Games. More recently, but particularly since the 1950s, many nations have recognised the importance of an effective coaching programme in a wide range of activities not only for the development of healthy participants but also for the kudos that success in major international events brings. One has only to look towards the 'eastern bloc' countries to see the value placed on success in sport. Vast sums of money have been lavished on facilities and on sportsmen and women to achieve the very highest standard. However, without the provision of competent coaches, any athlete's potential will never be fulfilled. Instrumental in producing these skilful performers is a comprehensive coach education programme.

There is a need for coaching at all levels of participation, from that of the reluctant novice to that of the Olympian. However, many sports and recreative activities have little in the way of a structured coaching programme. Furthermore, where they have existed, the effectiveness of such schemes has often been undermined by a failure to identify the performer's needs, the skills required by the coach and a structured coach education programme.

The Sports Council of Great Britain recognises around 160 individual sports and activities. Some of these have well-established coach education programmes and coaching structures; some do not. Currently there is little comparison in the various levels of coaching expertise between one sport and another. The terms used to identify the 'fount of all knowledge' tends to cloud the issue even more: coach, teacher, trainer, instructor, adviser and consultant spring immediately to mind. Do they mean the same thing? If not, what is the difference? Is 'a senior instructor' the same as 'an advanced coach'? Since the late 1970s there has been a move to develop a strategy for coach education in Great Britain that will not only lead to better educated coaches but will also standardise the various levels of expertise.

The need of late for internationally recognised standards of coaching ability has also emerged. The development of interest in all sports, recreation and leisure activities throughout the world has led to an increase in the mobility of participants and coaches. Most sports associations have a regular programme of visiting international teams and individuals competing against the host nation; similarly, they send representative teams and individuals abroad. With this involvement in the development of sporting excellence has come a regular interchange of coaching knowledge and expertise. There is now a desire amongst some coaches to work outside their home country, passing on their knowledge and skills to others.

The difficulty with this situation is how does a prospective employer in one country assess the validity of qualifications gained in another and the level of expertise that they reflect? Quite clearly there is a major problem. However, through the National Coaching Foundation in the United Kingdom a forum has been set up to attempt to standardise such qualifications for the benefit of all concerned.

It is a fact that there are many thousands of individuals who pass on their skills and knowledge to others. What is their experience and understanding of sport? The situation is far from clear in that coaches can have very different sporting backgrounds and reasons for coaching.

Who takes up coaching?

Former participants

Coaches in this category obviously have some degree of knowledge of the activity, but it will be coloured by their own experiences. At one extreme, they may be former champions and élite performers, and this in itself can create a major problem. Élite performers, by and large, are individuals who have a single-minded determination, dedication and commitment to succeed. They also possess a great deal of natural ability. For them, learning skills is easy, and they often find difficulty in relating to slow learners or less able individuals. Similarly, they find it hard to associate with others who are only seeking the recreative fun aspect of the activity.

Coaches who were 'enthusiastic participants' and were not necessarily successful tend, on the whole, to be more able to identify with the less gifted performer and the social, emotional and physical benefits of participation. However, by definition, they have little experience of the needs of élite performance. When one looks at the requirements of specific groups such as junior, female, male, elderly, disabled, socially disadvantaged, competitive, non-competitive, aggressive, shy, introverted or combinations of any or all of the above, many coaches have been, to say the least, under-prepared. However, the sporting background of a potential coach is not an indication of ability to communicate knowledge and skills in an effective and efficient manner.

The ideal coach is one who can help each individual to achieve his potential, no matter what the final level of performance might be. Former performers tend to emphasise that part of the activity that

The coach must be able to offer the individual every opportunity to achieve his potential. The coach must therefore possess the necessary skills and qualities

they enjoyed or found easy, or in which they were themselves skilful. Therefore, they may not be able, or want, to offer the wide range of skills and knowledge required by each participant. In addition, élite performers' narrow experience may be that which is required for specific individuals, but it may be inappropriate for most participants. Because a coach was once a very successful participant, it does not mean that he has the indepth knowledge and understanding of the activity or the personal, organisational and communication skills to help and advise others.

Parents

Many sports attract a large number of youngsters. There are activities, for example karate, that have as many as 80% of their participants under sixteen years of age. It is natural that some parents will develop an interest in the activity by association with their child's involvement. They may be former sportsmen themselves in that or another activity. On the other hand, they may have some specific expertise, as a doctor for example, and may want to become involved in the coaching process. They may wish to advise their own children or to coach within the club generally.

As non-practitioners there are obvious limitations to knowledge and skills that they can pass on to others. Having read a book or seen a video does not make someone an expert! So, the opportunity must be created for those interested in coaching to learn the techniques and tactics, and any other related knowledge, of the activity appropriate to their level of involvement.

There is also the problem of the overzealous parent seeking to relive former personal glory or to experience personal success through the efforts of his youngsters. Often the 'parent/coach' offers less than the ideal relationship: over-ambition for his children and a sense of personal affront if the child does not succeed. Children are very vulnerable both physically and mentally: they are physiologically unable to cope with intensive training and, perhaps more importantly, the emotional, social and personal pressures that they can find themselves subject to must not be underestimated. Youngsters can develop intense feelings of guilt if they think that they are letting down parents, relations, coaches and friends. With careful counselling, perhaps not to coach their own child, parents can be an invaluable resource. The problem, however, is that as their youngsters lose interest in the activity, so the parents are lost to the sport as well.

The future of any sport depends upon the careful nurturing of youngsters' talent and interest. If they can retain enthusiasm and, possibly with the gifted few, the ability to achieve excellence, the continued development of the activity is assured. They will remain active participants at whatever level they choose into their adult life. On the other hand, if their early experiences are associated with extreme physical and mental stress, they will very soon be lost to the sport and will develop negative attitudes to the benefits of physical exercise in general. Greater efforts must be made to ensure that when children, the lifeblood of any sport, are introduced to an activity, they are allowed to develop with the appropriate support and awareness of their needs. It has been suggested that coaches who are particularly well qualified should be involved at this level to avoid any insensitive or over-enthusiastic attention.

Friends

Friends of performers can be another source of help in coaching. At first, they will probably be involved only with their companion, but again with counselling they can be encouraged to help others. As with parents, they may have little or no knowledge of the activity and so, at least initially, will have limited technical experience. But with a carefully structured education programme they can have a very important role to play.

Physical educationalists

An obvious source of potential coaching expertise are those who have trained as physical education teachers. As experienced professionals they have the ability to pass on to and develop skills and knowledge with others who may have a different level of ability and commitment.

Though their initial training may be in introducing the general skills common to all physical activity, nevertheless in many cases they have indepth knowledge of specific activities, particularly those in which they have participated. Due to the nature of their employment, teachers tend to devote some of their free time to the development of sporting potential in their own school. As a result, they often have little, if any, time for coaching in sports clubs. They do, however, provide a most valuable service to all sport by introducing youngsters to physical activity and by creating opportunities for links between schools and clubs, which must benefit all concerned.

With the national and personal rewards of participation in physical activity becoming ever more important, the need for a comprehensive and indepth coaching programme has become paramount. In recent years, in an attempt to maximise sporting potential, doctors, pharmacologists, nutritionalists, physiologists, psychologists, educationalists, physicists and bio-mechanicians have made valued contributions to improving performance. Out of this pooling of information has emerged a body of knowledge that will maximise the effectiveness of the coach. It has been identified that all coaches do not have to be educated to the same level or develop expertise in similar areas. A nationally and internationally identified coaching structure has been developed that will allow coaches to contribute at whatever level their expertise or desire warrants. Although of course it is sound educational policy to follow such a programme, it is also obviously beneficial to both sport and participants by enabling them to achieve their objectives.

Who wants to be a coach?

There can be little doubt that in society there is an ever-increasing demand for 'value for money'. This philosophy does not deal only with the materialistic aspects of life such as 'consumer items' – clothes, cars, houses – but it also includes sport and leisure. If I buy a car I want value for money. It needs to meet all of the advertised economic and mechanical specifications and at the advertised price. Similarly, if I were to attend an educational, professional or vocational course that would give me the knowledge and understanding to acquire a qualification, I would expect to get that qualification. So, too, with coaching: if I give up my valuable free time, and pay to participate in a particular activity, I expect to learn and develop skills. It's all very well accepting the philosophical attitude that a person will develop as an individual through the training process, but unfortunately this alone is not good enough; we need to see results. Perhaps to satisfy our flagging egos and constantly ensure value for money, we need reassurance that we are improving. There is also the other aspect that sport offers potentially very lucrative career opportunities. If I want to earn a living as a footballer or tennis player, the coach must be able to allow me to reach the necessary standard.

It is no longer assumed that a coach's personal level of performance or area of interest will automatically enable him to be an effective teacher. (Where is the professional training programme that taught him the vital communication techniques for passing on knowledge to others?) Equally, an enthusiastic non-participant may want to coach but does not have the necessary technical knowledge. There are thousands of established coaches in sport and recreation, and many more who want to take on that role but who are unaware of the responsibilities and duties necessary for effective and efficient instruction.

The coach or aspiring coach has to ask himself some important questions about his motives for wanting to coach:

YOUR COACHING DUTIES	OTHER RESPONSIBILITIES
Instructor	Knowledge
Teacher	Enthusiasm
Trainer	Safety
Motivator	Discipline
Disciplinarian	Maturity
Social worker	Willingness
Friend	Respect
Scientist	Fairness
Student	Coolness
Manager	Recognition
Administrator	Support
Publicity agent	Good samaritan

The role of the coach

Being a coach is a privilege. It is vital, therefore, that any aspiring coach is fully aware of the demands and responsibilities that go with the honour

- who asked me to become a coach?
- what makes me think that I can coach?
- do I have the right technical skills to be a coach?
- are my communication skills good enough for me to be a coach?
- am I good at organising?
- do I have administration skills?
- do I have the right personal skills to be a coach?
- am I prepared to accept the responsibility of being a coach?

Society expects a certain standard of competence from 'experts'. The main question that coaches and potential coaches must ask themselves is quite simple: 'Do I have the necessary technical and communication skills to coach effectively?'

A coach's level of technical proficiency may be a measure of his personal experience, not of his ability to teach. The following sections will identiy the skills needed for a coach to be effective. If these skills are incorporated into a coaching programme that takes into account the coach's own personality, technical competence and knowledge of his sport, then a most productive teaching and learning environment will be created.

Coach education

There are two main problems with this proposition. Firstly there has been little, if any, comparability of technical competence between similar coaching grades in different activities and, secondly, there has been little 'quality control' over coaches' competence and effectiveness. A need has arisen both nationally and internationally for a self-regulatory body to agree acceptable good practice, various levels of technical competence and coaching standards.

Most sports governing bodies in the UK and throughout the world have identified four levels of coaching expertise. The National Coaching Foundation has suggested a similar structure.

However, from the start there has been more than a little resistance to a proposed coaching programme, and the concern has probably been justified. One of the biggest problems with the coach education programmes of the 160 or so governing bodies and associations recognised by the Sports Council lay in the simple fact that the greatest part of them had no requirement for a personal standard of performance. Putting it simply, it would be possible to become a national coach, let alone a coach at one of the lower levels, without ever having participated in the activity either as a competitor or as a performer. Activities such as athletics, swimming and gymnastics spring immediately to mind. All knowledge in terms of coaching in such activities can be purely theoretical and so the need for a comprehensive coach education programme is obvious, well-received and supported. However, in these programmes not all of the information is sport-specific; as much as 50% of the time is devoted to the development of management, communication and coaching skills. It is not enough to have a body of knowledge to be a successful coach. The ability to pass on those skills to others in such a way that all sportsmen, at whatever level, can achieve their potential is essential.

There are other activities, such as the martial arts and soccer, where an individual's personal level of competence has been the sole measure of his coaching ability. Coaching status has been awarded on that single criterion, even though communication skills may never have been explained, skills that might have improved teaching ability. With these particular groups coaching success has been based on trial and error! The many excellent coaches who have been instructing for years and who emerged from such potentially

The coach must ensure that any activities taught are appropriate to the individuals concerned .

unpromising situations have taught both good and bad lessons. They have learned what does and, more importantly, what does not work when teaching different 'types' of performer. It is among this group of coaches that a misunderstanding of a coach education programme has developed. There has been a notion of:

'I've been coaching for twenty years. What can they teach me?'

As has been identified, probably very little, if anything at all. In fact, if the coaches were to be exposed to any 'new' ideas it would be surprising. All that this group of coaches should pick up from any of the courses is confirmation that what they have identified as safe, efficient and effective coaching is actually recognised as good practice by academics and professional communicators. The whole purpose of any coach education programme is to short-circuit that potentially dangerous learning process by identifying to embryonic coaches good practice from the outset without exposing them to the possible pitfalls and dangers of a trial and error process of 'experimental learning'. It would be unthinkable for a parent to allow his child to be taught mathematics in school by someone who was not qualified to do so, or by a teacher who was learning by his mistakes as he went along, no doubt at the expense of the child. So, too, in sport everyone should have the opportunity to be coached by qualified personnel.

The international dimension
— • —

The status of coaches in many sports has never reflected their contribution to the development of the activity. Most coaches are amateurs in the truest sense of the word and give freely of their time for the benefit of others. Unfortunately this philanthropic state of affairs has directly resulted in their lack of status. Many coaches have attended coaching courses run by their governing body and specialist workshops at institutions of higher education. They have made a great commitment to the development of their coaching effectiveness in both time and money. Although they offer their services as amateurs they have a professional attitude to their duties and responsibilities. Obviously they will not have the same broad base of experience as a P.E. teacher, but in their own particular sport or activity their expertise is at least on a par and should be recognised as such.

Over the past few years the government has asked physical educationalists, coaches and sports governing bodies to examine the structure and content of physical education in schools. Out of their investigations and discussions has emerged an all-embracing programme of sporting development 'from the cradle to the grave'. In order to construct the 'National Strategy for Sport' four stages of sporting development have been identified.

The foundation period – up to seven years of age

Coaches and physical educationalists agree that children should be offered a broad range of non-specific physical activity. Children should not specialise in any one sport. Basic co-ordination skills and movement patterns should be developed to establish a broad-based 'foundation'.

The participation period – 7 to 11 years of age

Most sports were devised by men for men at the peak of their physical activity, so they are simply not suitable for children! It is not acceptable for children to play on the same size pitch as the adults', use the same equipment or adhere to the same rules as adults'. They have neither the physical nor the intellectual maturity to behave as

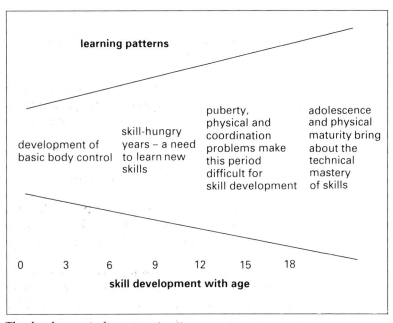

The development of movement patterns
All sports attract a large number of young participants. The coach must be aware of the way in which motor skills are developed

adults. During this period of physical development children should experience modified versions of adult games, activities designed to develop specific skills. Youngsters should be offered as wide a range of physical and sporting experience as possible.

The performance period – eleven to fourteen years of age

During this period, youngsters should be exposed to activities that have not been modified. By experiencing the full game situation in a wide range of activities, they will be able to appreciate the varied demands and benefits. The children will be able to identify which activities they are best suited to in physical, mental and personal enjoyment terms.

The development of excellence – fourteen to sixteen years of age

At this stage youngsters should be able to specialise in a particular sport if they wish. If offered a wide range of sporting experience, most children will be able to find at least one activity they are good at and which, with effort, could develop.

Specialisation – sixteen years of age and older

From the age of sixteen sportsmen are becoming physically and mentally more mature and are capable of withstanding the pressures of specialisation. They are able to identify for themselves the activity that they want to develop.

One of the biggest areas of misunderstanding centres around the idea that physical education in schools is not sport. It actually offers every pupil the opportunity to develop a broad base of motor skills on which to build future specialisation. The physical educationalist is the 'facilitator' of the learning of movement patterns for all pupils, not just for a gifted élite.

In the new structure for sporting development there will be an integrated school and club programme. The school will teach basic movement skills and co-ordination, and will introduce pupils to the various sports. The clubs will offer the opportunity to develop those skills. Teachers possess an understanding of the introduction of motor skills to all pupils, whereas coaches possess specific technical and tactical knowledge. With a few exceptions, teachers and coaches do not have a knowledge and understanding of each other's areas, but together they can create opportunities for the sporting development of all interested individuals.

There is an interesting aspect to this situation that might not immediately be obvious. Coaches may have to take on more of the physical educationalist's role. They may have to introduce basic motor skills and develop co-ordination, very much in the same way as is done in schools. The coach must not see his role merely as a developer of specialised sporting excellence, but as covering both aspects. He should seek the help and advice of the physical educationalist if he is to develop those pedagogical skills. Similarly, the physical educationalist can learn sports specific knowledge from coaches. For the best learning and teaching environment there is going to be a need for a great sharing of expertise, which will create a mutually beneficial relationship between sport and physical education.

A standardised coaching structure

Membership of the European Community has highlighted two major problems with coaching qualifications. Firstly there is a disparity in the level of expertise between coaches in different sports operating at the same level. Secondly, in the European dimension, how does one know whether, for example, an Italian coach is qualified or what his level of coaching expertise is?

Over the last few years sports governing bodies and government agencies have been discussing the problem of a nationally and internationally recognised coaching award. Although there have been many contentious areas of debate, a broad structure has been produced. This single, simple standardised coaching structure, linked to a nationally recognised qualification, will be of immense value to governing bodies, local authority facility providers, employers, sportsmen and parents.

Sports administrators and national training agencies have been involved in devising a five-tier coaching structure that will be awarded the status of a National Vocational Qualification (NVQ). There are primarily four levels of coaching accreditation, which are attainable by any committed coach, and an 'extra' fifth level that identifies more of the design, organisation and administration of a coaching programme at a national level. The structure of the fifth level is very similar to a Physical Education, Sports Science or Leisure Management degree. The nationally recognised validation will have different names in different countries, but the content and standard of each of the five levels will be the same.

The main thrust of the NVQ is to accentuate personal competence and an underpinning knowledge of the skills. The validating structure is based upon the ability to coach, rather than on academic qualifications. However, the importance of coaching theory is not forgotten; this is brought in where appropriate at the higher levels.

A National Vocational Qualification will identify the competence of a coach in terms of his technical and tactical knowledge, and his

Rockclimbing, like any other sport or leisure activity, requires a coach's skills and knowledge for the development of technical competence

ability to communicate skills. For example, a coach with a level one NVQ will have a basic knowledge and understanding of his sport and a limited ability to express them to others, whereas a level four coach will have an indepth understanding and knowledge of his sport and will be able to use his skills in a wide range of situations.

The agencies involved in devising this nationally and internationally recognised coaching qualification have had to define their terms of reference in order to standardise the structure.

NVQ

National Vocational Qualification relevant to employment which attests the current competence of the holder. It is a statement of an individual's competence to perform a range of activities and implies skills, underpinning knowledge and understanding.

The various NVQ levels identify the degree of competence, knowledge and understanding. The requirement for current coaching involvement will prevent those individuals who obtained a qualification many years previously, or who have not been involved recently, from being automatically regarded as competent. Governing bodies must keep a register of current coaches and devise a programme of updating in line with new trends in coaching, and technical and tactical theory. This programme must also provide the means by which old qualifications can be updated.

Sport

Any sport or physical activity.

Any activity, whether competitive, like soccer and athletics, non-competitive, like aerobics and tai chi chuan, is classified as 'sport'.

Coach

Anyone who coaches, teaches or gives instruction but who is not a full-time education professional or an administrative director of coaching.

This definition identifies the fact that physical educationalists are the experts in developing basic movement skills, co-ordination and an understanding of the principles of a wide range of sports, but that by and large they do not have an underlying specialist knowledge and understanding of a particular activity. So, unless they have a specific coaching qualification, they will not be recognised as coaches. Furthermore, individuals who hold administrative posts in sporting organisations cannot claim to be a coach unless they have a current coaching qualification.

Coaching

The process of imparting techniques, skills, knowledge and attitudes which is aimed at improving the performance of the individuals by using methods appropriate to their ability and aspirations.

This definition clearly states the all-embracing role of the coach. It is not about identifying and developing an élite few to obtain national or international status for a governing body and a coach; rather it makes provision for sporting development in every potential performer.

For further clarification it might be useful to identify the levels of coaching competence as validated by NVQ.

Level 1

At this level the coach should be competent in coaching basic, routine and predictable activities. This level of competence identifies his technical ability and his level of experience in communicating his understanding and knowledge of his sport. In practice, he will assist the session coach by taking part of the lesson or class in routine practices under supervision and guidance. Experience gained at this level acts as a foundation for future progression.

Level 2

The coach should display competence in a wide range of activities. He should be able to take a session on his own without constant supervision. He must, of course, possess the appropriate knowledge to be able to meet the needs of each group member.

Level 3

At this level the coach should display a deeper understanding of the skills required for more complex activities. He should be able to take the responsibility for the planning, organisation, administration and setting of coaching standards for an individual session or club. So, he obviously needs to have the knowledge and skills to cope with all his club members' needs, as well as administrative ability to ensure the success of his club.

Level 4

The coach should display competence in the more technically demanding activities of his sport. He must possess administrative and organisational skills to facilitate the development of his sport, club and individual athletes in his care. He also needs sound managerial skills, together with a sense of responsibility for the successful development of the sport – he may have some local or regional responsibility.

Obviously in the construction of such a validating process generalisations have had to be made. They may not suit each sport or every coach's particular needs, but they do form a useful standardised structure to work to. In trying to reconcile a large number of different activities – e.g. soccer, gymnastics, athletics and potholing – there has to be a degree of give and take. However, despite any drawbacks, NVQ will offer for the first time an opportunity for coaches to receive the status in society that their skills and commitment richly deserve.

The following chapters identify the skills and knowledge that the coach will require under the terms of NVQ. In many cases what is described is already identified as good practice in many sports. The wheel cannot be reinvented! In some instances a more wide-ranging description of coaching skills might be presented. It is for the individual coach to identify those elements that are relevant to his needs and sport. For example, some sports do not attract children; therefore, an understanding of the effect of sport on this group may be academic. Devising a training programme to bring about peak performance in a competition, or similar assessment situation, may not be appropriate in non-competitive activities. However, it does not mean to say that such knowledge is of no benefit to the coach, especially in producing progressive schedules!

Coaches must ensure that they are aware of any specific governing body requirements for the level of NVQ for which they are preparing.

A coach education programme

The demands of coaching are far removed from the traditional image of the ex-player or the enthusiastic amateur trying to pass his skills and knowledge on to others. The expectations of participants in terms of quality and delivery of instruction are now far higher than they were in the past. And quite rightly so! From the governing body's point of view and that of those responsible for trying to run a financially viable club, quality coaching and effective presentation of an activity will attract the general public.

The content of the courses leading to awards has been discussed at length. There is really little opportunity for great variations in structure and content, as there has to be comparability with and a commonality between sports governing body awards at each level. Good coaching practice in one sport has very similar requirements to good coaching in another. The techniques may be different, but the communication, organisational and management skills required to create the best teaching and learning environment are much the same.

The aim of a coach education programme is to identify an efficient and effective system of coaching. Fundamental to this are, of course, the individual governing bodies' participation and competition structure, and the internal means of athlete and coach development. Both of these factors may have a profound effect on the teaching situation. Without being too specific, the following guidelines identify some of the features that are identified as good practice in current coaching programmes.

They include the following elements.

Assessment of:
1   the varied requirements and expectations of the participants, including age, gender, ability and general health
2   the differing physical and psychological demands of each sport

3   the differing physical and psychological demands of training, progress evaluation and the competitive environment
4   current trends in techniques, tactics, training, assessment and competition
5   current policy within the governing body specifically and sport and leisure in general.

Planning the programme, including:
6   long-term training to allow participants of all abilities to achieve their potential
7   making the fullest use of available technical and facility resources
8   keeping accurate records on the development of participants and being aware of specific dates and information that might influence the training programme.

Implementing the programme:
9   organise and monitor the long-term coaching programme for each participant
10   plan and teach individual lessons that make up the programme
11   develop communication skills with athletes and all other personnel involved
12   create and develop personal and professional relationships with other individuals and organisations
13   manage facilities and other coaches to facilitate the implementation of the coaching programme.

Analysing the programme by:
14   being able to analyse constructively each training, assessment or competition session
15   being able to analyse constructively the work of other coaches and organisations
16   being able to analyse constructively the effectiveness of the overall coaching programme.

All of the above elements are common to most sports and leisure activities. For individual sports the units can be grouped in various ways.

General and specific knowledge of sport:
•   the present structure of the sport nationally and internationally

- the philosophy and traditions of the sport
- the place of sport in society
- the recruitment pattern of participants
- provision of resources for effective teaching and learning.

The benefits of participation in sport
Is this considered within the total life-style of the participant?

Organisation and administration
Coaches should recognise the importance of:
- devising and implementing a long-term training programme
- establishing and maintaining standards of dress, behaviour, attitude, and commitment to participants
- implementing safety regulations and accident procedures
- ensuring regular tuition
- devising a system to reward excellence and impose sanction where appropriate
- arranging extra training where appropriate
- arranging for assessment and competitions
- ordering equipment for participants
- arranging and managing training camps and competition trips and tours
- communicating with governing bodies, the media and other agencies
- acting as a representative on committees and at meetings.

Staffing and the coach education programme

- knowledgeable, interested and committed coaches will greatly influence the development of an association
- in-house association or governing body courses
- courses run by outside agencies
- developmental needs
- association needs.

The coach education programme should be both comprehensive and structured to include all of the necessary elements to produce efficient, effective and safe training, assessment and competition. As previously identified, the programme falls into four levels of coaching competence. The fifth level is intended for those few coaches who will have an input into the national structure of the sport. The outline programmes of coaching competence described in the following sections are aimed primarily at the majority of coaches who work at club, local and, possibly, regional levels.

1 A FOUNDATION COURSE COVERING BASIC COACHING SKILLS

This is for the aspiring coach on the first rung of the coaching ladder who will assist the class or session coach. The first level of coaching involves 'work place' experience under the watchful eye of a senior coach where the embryonic coach will develop the ability to:
- work closely with and under the supervision of the class coach
- demonstrate and explain basic techniques
- identify errors and suggest methods of correction
- give feedback to the participants
- reinforce good performance with praise
- adapt a teaching style to suit different situations
- develop an effective working relationship with participants
- ensure maximum participation and enjoyment
- prepare participants for training
- cool down participants after training.

There will also be a requirement for the candidate to 'log' his coaching activities, which will be monitored by suitably qualified personnel.

2 A BASIC COACHING AWARD

After gaining both experience and confidence the aspiring coach might want to develop the skills required to teach a class without the constant supervision of another coach. The following elements should be considered:
- where does the club fit into the national structure?
- what does the coach do?
- how does the coach behave?
- the coach's responsibility
- how to screen new students

Polevaulting is an extremely complicated skill. However, even a basic coaching award can be sufficient to enable an athlete to achieve a reasonable performance

- the whys and wherefores of warm-up and cool-down
- training safety
- how to coach
- what insurance does and does not cover
- how to deal with emergencies.

Again, the candidate will be required to log his coaching activities, which will be monitored by suitably qualified personnel.

3 AN INTERMEDIATE COACHING AWARD

For those coaches who want to improve their coaching abilities further, for example run their own clubs, a third level of coaching accreditation is available, covering the following topics:

- how to get the best from your athletes (the teaching of skills)
- how to measure ability (fitness)
- how to improve performance (fitness)
- how to counsel participants over training set-backs
- how to coach children and young participants
- how to deal with setbacks
- working with specific groups and injured athletes
- how to set targets and plan training
- opening, promoting and developing a club
- managing the club
- organising courses and events.

The candidate will log his coaching activities, which will be monitored by suitably qualified personnel.

4 AN ADVANCED COACHING AWARD

For those coaches who aspire to the highest levels of coaching there is a course specifically for them that covers the following units:

- the philosophy of coaching sport
- the development of technical excellence
- the development of mobility
- the development of strength
- the development of speed
- the development of endurance
- the biomechanical analysis of technique
- nutrition
- factors affecting performance
- planning the programme.

This course is organised closely with individual governing bodies to facilitate an evaluation of the candidates':

- personal, technical competence

- assessement and grading skills
- teaching of advanced techniques
- preparation of students for assessment or competition.

The exact content and direction of each level of coaching competence and the content of courses organised by governing bodies may vary from the format suggested here. However, any course and level of coaching competence will cover all of the topics identified, since they are the essential elements of good coaching irrespective of the activity, although the emphasis might vary.

Requirements of governing bodies may differ from sport to sport and are constantly being reviewed in the light of current trends in technical development, sports science and legislation. Governing bodies may require specific knowledge or make particular demands on coaches, so it is essential that aspiring coaches are fully aware of current thinking.

There are some very obvious benefits to be obtained from the implementation of a national or international coaching structure:

1 it offers one nationally recognised set of coaching accreditation for all sports
2 the levels of coaching competence are comparable with all sports governing bodies and associations
3 the structure of the awards and course content recognise the personal technical competence and involvement in the chosen sport
4 the structure of each award level is linked closely to the individual governing body's and association's own levels of technical competence, experience and ability
5 the structure offers a clear pathway to coaching and developing a coaching hierarchy.

The following example of a framework for a coach education programme should be seen as simply that. It is not meant to be prescriptive or inclusive, but simply a basis for the development of good coaching practice. For instance an association might want to devise a programme for coaches primarily involved with youngsters under the age of sixteen. Obviously the four levels of competence and their units remain more or less the same, but there would be an indepth study of their application to youngsters. A similar fourth level of coaching can always be devised to meet special needs groups, such as the elderly or physically disadvantaged. Governing bodies or associations are at liberty to add on sport-specific material at the appropriate level. But any coaching programme must include the common elements that are a prerequisite of good practice, irrespective of the sport.

I have attempted to identify in a very skeletal fashion the individual elements of the different levels. They are not meant in any way to be absolute but a guide for more detailed development as required. It would be the hope that each sport and activity would develop each unit specifically while at the same time encompassing the common elements required for good practice. The Assistant, Coach and Senior Awards follow this pattern; however, the Advanced Coach Award will be so sport-specific that it is difficult to describe anything other than a generic framework.

Assistant Coach Award

1 Work closely with the class coach

The Assistant Coach, as the name implies, operates as an assistant to the coach in charge of the lesson. He carries out duties as directed by the coach and is always under his control. The Assistant Coach is not qualified to take a class without the supervision of a suitably qualified coach. It is obvious that the class coach and his assistant will be quite clear about their duties and responsibilities, and will create a positive working relationship.

2 Demonstrate and explain techniques and tactics

When required by the coach in charge, the Assistant Coach should be able to organise a demonstration by himself, or by using another participant or visual material, for example film or video. The demonstration, however devised, must be organised so that all of the participants have a clear view. It is equally important that key points of technique, aspects of safety and organisational details are clearly identified. To enable students to understand fully what is expected of them there must be an opportunity for questions to be asked and answered.

3 Identify errors in techniques and tactics

It is not enough to identify poor techniques or tactics; participants need to know how they can be corrected.

4 Give feedback to the students

Training and competition can be counterproductive if athletes are not made aware of their good or bad performance. They need to know if their efforts are correct. Bad practice can engrain bad technique.

5 Reinforce good performance with praise

It is only human nature to want to be successful in anything. Performers need to have the encouragement of their coach and others when they are working well. Even with poor technique or performance there has to be something positive that the coach can praise. Too much negative criticism can be detrimental to the performance of an individual.

6 Adapt a teaching style to suit different situations

The Assistant Coach must be adaptable in his style of presentation and organisation, depending on whether he is dealing with large and small groups or individuals. He must also change the tone and volume of his voice to meet his style of presentation.

7 Develop an effective working relationship with students

All students are different! They each respond to a particular style of presentation in dissimilar ways. The Assistant Coach has to identify the appropriate style for each performer.

8 Ensure maximum participation and enjoyment

Not all athletes have the same degree of motivation or commitment. Some are recreational and social participants, others are committed competitors. The Assistant Coach must ensure that all participants are working at a level that is appropriate to them individually.

COACH EDUCATION PROGRAMME
COACHING ASSESSMENT

LEVEL – ASSISTANT/COACH/SENIOR/ADVANCED

OVERALL ABILITY

Coach's Name ....

Association/Governing Body ....

Assessor .... Date ....

Level of confidence	A	B	C	D	E
Communication skills					
Verbal	A	B	C	D	E
Non-verbal	A	B	C	D	E
Awareness of current good practice	A	B	C	D	E
Attitude	A	B	C	D	E
Interesting personality	A	B	C	D	E
Sense of humour	A	B	C	D	E
Presence	A	B	C	D	E
Maturity	A	B	C	D	E
Awareness of specific groups					
Males/Females	A	B	C	D	E
Children	A	B	C	D	E
Mature	A	B	C	D	E
Elite	A	B	C	D	E
Club	A	B	C	D	E
Disadvantaged	A	B	C	D	E

A = Excellent   B = Good   C = Satisfactory   D = Poor   E = Fail

COACHING SKILLS

Introduction of: techniques/tactics activity and application	A	B	C	D	E
Demonstration: visibility whole/part speed	A	B	C	D	E
Explanation: coaching points/ whole/part practice points	A	B	C	D	E
Activity: appropriate/ organisation/ feedback/ effective	A	B	C	D	E
Summary: key points	A	B	C	D	E
Organisation: students' space for safe practice	A	B	C	D	E
Use of voice: appropriate to Class	A	B	C	D	E
Groups	A	B	C	D	E
Individuals	A	B	C	D	E

General observations

Overall Grade _____

Signature of Assessor _____

A = Excellent   B = Good   C = Satisfactory   D = Poor   E = Fail

Coaching assessment

All coaches need a wide array of personal and communication skills. The essentials of good coaching are common to all activities. The 'check-off' list indicates many of the common elements of good practice

9 Prepare students for training

It is essential that athletes 'warm up' in a systematic and progressive manner that is appropriate to their fitness and to the following physical activity. Any such preparation should include both physiological and psychological activities.

10 Cool down students after training

It is equally important that students 'cool down' after physical activity so that their physical and mental states are brought back down to that required for a 'normal' lifestyle.

COACH
—•—
AWARD

UNIT 1
The national structure of the sport

1 The chain of responsibility

This must be maintained in order to sustain quality instruction and high levels of technical competence in any governing body.

The Assistant Coach is responsible to the Club Coach, who in turn is responsible to the Senior Coach and then to the Advanced Coach, and on to local, regional, national and international governing body committees and organisations. Since there is a constant updating of approved techniques, training and coaching procedures such a structure offers a mechanism by which all coaches can be made aware of current good practice.

2 The role of the governing bodies

The governing body, with its various committees and levels of operation, is responsible for the standards of technical excellence and coaching of its members within the broad guidelines of its identified philosophy.

3 The role of a Director of Coaching

The Director of Coaching is responsible for ensuring that there is continued improvement in the standards of coaches and thereby in the overall standard of performance of members. The governing body is responsible for arranging national, regional and local courses, events and competitions that will further provide an opportunity to assess the continued development of a sport.

4 The national sporting structure

Each sport has representatives at a national level on the Sports Council or the Central Council for Physical Recreation. Its governing body is responsible for its members' conduct within such national and international organisations.

THE NATIONAL AND INTERNATIONAL STRUCTURE OF SPORT

Olympic Games   World Championships

International Championships

National Championships

Regional Championships

County Championships

City Championships

Club Championships

Most, if not all, sports have a well-developed national and international organisation

5 The development of policy within the sport

Most governing bodies provide a forum for their members and associated individuals from which to devise general policy.

6 The maintenance of standards in technical competence

It is the responsibility of a governing body to:
- set its own standard for technical competence
- identify approved techniques and good practice
- devise rules and regulations for competition
- implement a qualitative programme of assessment.

7 Comparative standards of technical and coaching competence

Each governing body is responsible for regulating its own activities.

8 The financial structure of the sport

The funding of clubs and governing bodies varies from sport to sport. Some activities rely on membership and training charges; others are 'free', but are dependent on grants from national, regional and local bodies.

9 The provision of information

The success of any activity depends on its ability to give the appropriate information and advice to prospective participants.

10 The availability and provision of grant aid

It is essential that governing bodies and coaches liaise with and make the fullest use of funding agencies.

UNIT 2
The role of the coach

1 The individual experiences of each coach in the sport

All coaches will be influenced by their own experience of their sport. Their enthusiasm, attitude, commitment and outlook on coaching will reflect their personal enjoyment and success in training and competition.

Those practices that they liked and to which they ascribed particular value and importance as students will in turn be emphasised in their training sessions. The way in which they carry out their various duties will also, to a degree, reflect their own coach's methods (although their personality will modify the activities they teach).

2 The common philosophy of coaches

No matter what their personal experiences, coaches should have a common philosophy about the benefits of participation in a sport; for example, it offers the opportunity for individuals to develop self-confidence, social skills and technical excellence, to improve their health and well-being, and to achieve success in competition. Ambitions and values should be in line with those of the governing body.

3 The need for coaches to keep up to date with current practice

All organisations are constantly reviewing their training, techniques and tactics in line with developments in sports science. It is therefore essential that coaches keep abreast of current good practice.

4 The need for coaches to be involved with the total development of their athletes

Coaches teach people, not techniques and tactics. They must understand that sport is only a part of a person's lifestyle and that the role sport plays in life must always be kept in perspective. Since the coach is a model for his students, it is important that he adopts a life style in and out of lessons that is appropriate to his 'professional' status. He must be prepared to spend time outside training supporting individuals with whom he works.

5 Within the philosophy of each sport the coach must meets the needs of the participants

Some sports are mainly competition-orientated, whereas others have no competitions at all on their calendar. The coach obviously has to work within the general philosophy of his sport, but at the same time he must attend to the needs of each of his students. Individual idiosyncrasies should be taken into account if he is to offer specific personal development. An athlete can improve, if only in a limited fashion, without direction, but a coach cannot function without students.

6 There is a need to look outside a sport to appreciate the contribution made by other activities

Forums now exist for the exchange of knowledge and experience (NCF and BISC are examples). It is realised that useful ideas can be gleaned from a number of different sources, which all help towards creating the optimum learning situation for each student. The conscientious coach is always willing to add to his knowledge, not only for his own personal interest and satisfaction, but also to improve the quality and effectiveness of his efforts.

7 A coach's views will be markedly influenced by his own experiences and understanding of his sport

The quality or lack of experience within a sport will obviously influence the coach's perspective.

8 The coach must be prepared to keep his technical and related knowledge up to date to promote effective coaching

A coach must be responsible for ensuring that he is aware of and implements current good practice, and it will probably require an investment of time and money. Evidence of the adoption and implementation of current knowledge may be a prerequisite for continued accreditation.

9 The coach must accurately assess each student's expectations of participation in the sport

In planning an individual programme for his athletes, the coach must evaluate most carefully their aspirations. All coaches, consciously or otherwise 'pigeon hole' participants by classifying their ability and commitment.

- The coach has to be able to assess accurately the physical and psychological potential of a student.
- The coach must be able to plan a progressive programme that will allow each participant to realise his ambitions.

10 What are the rewards that maintain the enthusiasm of both participant and coach?

The coach has to identify clearly short-, intermediate and long-term targets for himself and the participants. Only by being honest and realistic can he work out targets that will hold his students' and his own interest. Improvements in performance, technical excellence, general health and well-being, and financial rewards are all perfectly valid targets or rewards. The coach must ensure that these are achieved in order to maintain keenness and commitment.

UNIT 3
How the coach behaves

1 The appearance and conduct of the coach

Participants can learn a great deal from 'non-verbal' messages. If the coach thinks that appearance, dress, cleanliness, good manners and personal conduct are important, then he must be the example for his athletes to copy.

How the coach behaves
The coach must adopt a style of communication which is appropriate to the needs of the student(s) and particular situation(s)

2 The organisation of lessons

Each lesson must be carefully structured to achieve its objectives and to be in line with good teaching. A lesson that seems to move smoothly from activity to activity in a progressive and sequential manner may hide a great amount of careful thought and preparation. It is clearly essential that an acceptable routine of training is achieved.

A typical training session might follow these lines:
- introductory address or comments
- general warm-up
- introductory activities, special exercises or games
- revision of the previous session's main points or techniques
- new techniques or activities
- class/group/partner/individual activities
- concluding activities
- cool-down
- concluding address or comments.

Good training habits are an indication not only of a mature attitude towards a sport, but also of a well-organised and balanced life style.

3 Planning the programme of work

Each lesson must be a logical part of a progressive work programme. It must be appropriate to all individuals, to their ability, age, gender and level of commitment. Every lesson must fulfil two quite distinct criteria:
1 it must meet the requirements of skill and performance development that have been identified for that stage in the programme
2 it must allow each student to experience success and enjoyment in the various aspects of participation and to develop those values seen to be appropriate.

4 The coach's concern for and sensitivity towards his students

The coach must show a genuine interest in the technical and physical development of his students, as well as in their psychologi-

Date	Time	Venue	Number in class
	Duration		Age range
Aim of lesson			Males Females
Special points to note			

	Organisation	Teaching safety points
Introductory activities		
Development		
Conclusion		

Comments

Planning lessons

All lessons must have a structure and a purpose. Typically, a training session must have an introduction, development and conclusion. The selection and structure of activities will be specific to individual sports cal, social and emotional maturation. The student should feel that his coach is interested in him personally and in his sporting development.

5 The coach's manner towards students

The coach must develop a positive manner towards all of his athletes that is pleasant and appropriate to individuals and to the situation.

6 The need for activity in a lesson

Most, if not all, sports participants take part because they like physical exercise. Coaches should ensure that they are active within the lesson for as long as possible at their own level of ability.

7 Understanding the learning process

Coaches must be aware of how students develop physical and intellectual skills. Not all students learn in the same way or as quickly, so a more individualistic approach might be necessary with those experiencing problems.

8 How to use initiative

Coaches must be able to use their initiative in deviating from the lesson plan. However, they have a responsibility to their students to cover the core content of a lesson. Too many 'spontaneous' lessons will leave the athletes behind in their preparations.

9 The role of the coach as a psychologist

In understanding the needs of participants, how they respond to styles of teaching and their general behaviour, the coach has to operate as an amateur psychologist. However, he must know his limitations.

DRIBBLING RELAY RACE

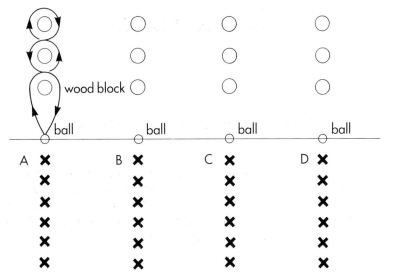

Specific practices
More detailed sketches and notes might be required for complicated activities

10 The role of the coach as a physiologist

If the coach is to bring about the required amount of physical adaptation, he must understand the way in which the body reacts to physical activity.

UNIT 4
How to coach

1 The personal standards of the coach must be exemplary

Athletes learn initially by mimicking their coach. In many instances he is the example to which they aspire. Participants see the coach as epitomising all that they want out of the activity: technique, appearance, attitude, determination, level of commitment, aspirations and personal values are all focused upon.

2 The coach must be able to explain precisely what he wants students to do

The coach must alter his voice accordingly to suit each situation. He must give clear, precise and succinct instruction. To be able to express ideas and concepts, and to place in the mind of a participant the image that a coach has in his own mind using the spoken word, is a skill to be cultivated.

3 The coach must be able to show the students what he wants them to do

In a class, group or individual demonstration the coach must be able to show students what is required. This might involve personal demonstration or using another participant, videos, films, books and charts.

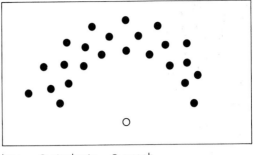

key   ● students   ○ coach

Demonstrations
The coach must set demonstrations so that all of the participants can clearly see. The organisation of any demonstration will be influenced by the size of the group, the complexity of the skill and the venue

4 The coach must be able to analyse students' attempts at a required technique

It is one of the essentials of good teaching that the coach is able to differentiate between good and bad practice. It is vital that those elements associated with excellence of performance are identified. The coach must act like a human video camera and be able to analyse the actions that he observes. Direct feedback should be given to the participants.

5 The coach must be sensitive to the individual learning difficulties of participants

Not all students learn as quickly as each other or in the same way. The coach must be aware of the idiosyncratic learning processes of each student and must devise practices to meet their needs. One of the essentials of good practice is to be able to recognise when someone is having problems, either outside of or in training.

6 The coach must be able to arrange instruction in whatever is required

In addition to highly specific skill development, most sports need a broad preparation base. It might involve fitness, tactics or psycho-

52

The approachable coach
The coach must be sensitive to every individual and to their particular needs, and must create a positive working relationship with each person

logical strategies. The coach must be able to facilitate the development of the athlete either by himself or by using others' skills.

7 The coach must not only plan the training carefully, but he must also record the progress of each student

If training is not monitored on a regular basis, how does the coach and athlete know that progress is being made? Furthermore, if there are positive or negative developments, this will give the coach immediate feedback about which training regime does or does not work. Special note should be taken of an individual's response to his programme that should be designed to take him lesson by lesson, week by week to achieve a particular standard. Note should also be taken of strengths and weaknesses that need attention.

8 Each lesson must be a logical element of the overall training strategy

A lesson must be seen as a building block in an overall training strategy aimed at developing an athlete's competence. Placed correctly, all lessons will contribute towards a progressive and systematic development programme. Placed incorrectly, and the result will be badly prepared athletes.

9 The coach must attempt to identify the motives of participants to allow them to achieve their expectations

As the amateur psychologist, the coach must identify each students' aspirations. He must also be prepared to vary his coaching style, being dictator, bully, disciplinarian, friend or confidant as the situation demands.

10 The coach must be able to devise progressive and systematic training programmes to allow athletes to fulfil their potential

The coach must have an understanding of the 'S' factors: speed, strength, suppleness, stamina, skill and 'p'sychology. Appreciating how the body adapts to training will enable the coach to devise personal programmes.

UNIT 5

How to assess new students

1 All students must complete a comprehensive application form prior to training

It is important that basic personal, health and sport related information is obtained.

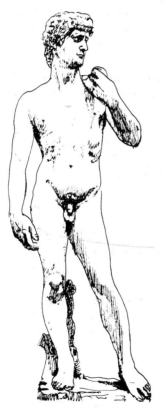

Not all students will possess the physical perfection and latent athletic potential of 'David' as depicted by Michelangelo

ACCIDENT REPORT

Date _____

Name of injured person _____

Address _____

_____ Phone _____

Time _____

Course activity and course no. _____

Non-course – why here? _____

Instructor's Report

1 PRECISE LOCATION
2 NATURE OF INJURY
3 NAMES OF WITNESSES

_____ Phone (   ) _____

_____ Phone (   ) _____

_____ Phone (   ) _____

4 ACTION TAKEN
   (a) You gave first aid   YES/NO   Are you
qualified?   YES/NO
   (b) First aid given by _____ qualified?   YES/NO
   (c) Called Doctor   YES/NO
   (d) Called Ambulance   YES/NO   Time called _____
   (e) Taken to Hospital by   _____
   (f) Hospital Action   _____

Signed _____
     by Injured person

Date   _____

              Staff Signature: _____

An accident report form
There is a need to record and report any accident. Some organisations might
wish to add particular elements or procedures

Such information should reveal whether a student is suffering from:

- diabetes
- epilepsy
- haemophilia
- asthma, hay fever or other general respiratory disorder
- heart disease
- physical disability
- recent injury
- other medical conditions that might affect participation.

It should also allow for details of prescribed or non-prescribed medication currently being taken.

All information must be treated in absolute confidence. If there are any doubts about a student's ability to train, a doctor's advice should be sought.

First aid
Accurate assessment of an injury and initial treatment speeds up the recovery process

UNIT 6
— • —
Warm-up and cool-down

1 The warm-up must be appropriate to each student

The coach must make allowances for age, gender and ability. The intensity and duration will be closely related to the participants' level of fitness.

2 The warm-up must be progressive

The warm-up must take the participant gradually from the normal demands of his daily life to that required by the sport. The warm-up should begin with 'whole body' activity and then be followed by more specific exercise that is related to the following training.

3 The warm-up must prepare the student psychologically for training

It is not a normal part of daily life to participate in intense physical activity and to adopt the mental commitment to do it. Participants need to create a particular state of mind and to maintain mental discipline in order to endure the rigours of training and competition.

4 The warm-up is an opportunity for mental rehearsal

The student should be encouraged to visualise the techniques (maybe as him performing them), tactics or activity to be practised. Research indicates that such imagery can facilitate the learning and teaching process.

5 The warm-up must be sufficient to raise the metabolic rate

The rate at which various chemical reactions take place in the body is dependent upon temperature. Within a very tight limitation of 1 degree Celsius increase in body temperature, i.e. from 37 to 38 degrees Celsius, there is an overall increase in energy availability of approximately 14%. However, such improvements may not be apparent for many physiological and psychological reasons. There is a great danger that participants will 'overwarm', which will cause the level of performance to deteriorate rapidly.

6 There are physiological implications of a warm-up in terms of increase of performance

All of the various chemical reactions and body efficiency are improved: the rate at which oxygen is made available to tissue and waste products are removed; muscle contraction and relaxation; and nerves carry messages to the brain faster, thereby decreasing reaction time. Recent research indicates an overall improvement of 5% in performance due to a thorough warm-up.

7 The warm-up has an effect upon the development of fatigue

The increase in the rate of chemical reactions improves the breakdown and removal of waste products, which are often a contributory factor in fatigue. A thorough cool-down will ensure that no waste remains in tissues after the session.

8 The warm-up can have a specific effect on the 'S' factors: speed, strength, stamina, suppleness, skill and 'p'sychology

As the warm-up progresses from the general to the specific, any individual 'S' factor must be suitably prepared. The warm-up must be specific to the demands of the activity.

9 The warm-up has a role to play in the prevention of injury

Systematic and progressive loading of connective tissue can reduce the risk of injury: tissues are gradually prepared for ever more intensive work loads and so are more likely to withstand the great stresses placed on them. They are therefore less likely to be damaged. Increased blood flow during warm-up, activity and cool-down helps to remove waste products, which are often associated with muscle soreness and which inhibit the recovery and repair process.

10 The effect of relaxation during the 'cool-down' phase

A relaxed body is able to recover from physical activity and adapt to the training load much faster than one that is not.

UNIT 7

Insurance cover

1 The importance of students' insurance cover

It is essential that in the event of an accident or injury a student can receive the appropriate financial compensation.

2 What does insurance cover?

It should cover, at the very least, death, the loss of a limb, permanent disability, loss of earnings and incidental expenses, such as medical treatment. The ability to claim for personal loss, such as money, jewellery, equipment and clothes should also be available.

3 The benefits for the unemployed and students

Most insurance has the same capital cover for the unemployed and students as for other people, but reduced benefit for loss of earnings.

4 Participant to participant insurance cover

In some of the contact sports there is a need for cover to cater for possible injury caused by physical contact in the course of training or competition.

5 Dental insurance cover

In many contact sports dental insurance is an added extra to normal cover.

6 Junior students

Junior students are normally eligible for reduced capital and earnings-related benefits.

7 The commencement of insurance cover

In some sports it is a prerequisite that insurance cover is arranged before participation.

8 Professional indemnity

Any coach, whether professional or amateur, should ensure that he has sufficient insurance cover in case a claim is made against him.

9 Negligence

In the case of negligence on the part of the coach, it is essential that he has the appropriate insurance cover.

10 How to make a claim

Most organisations have a formal claims procedure. It is incumbent upon the organisation to make known such a procedure to all of its coaches.

UNIT 8
—•—
How to deal with emergencies

1 The importance of effective first aid

The coach should be aware of the value of first aid and it is obviously advantageous if he is a qualified First Aider. Assistance should only be rendered by suitably qualified personnel. Any first aid administered should simply be a means of keeping the injured athlete as comfortable as possible until the appropriate medical treatment is given either by the emergency services or by suitably qualified medical practitioners.

2 The importance of an initial and accurate assessment of the injury

The first aider should remain calm, and should reassure the injured athlete and any others in the group. If unsure of the exact nature of the injury, err on the side of caution and expect the worst! If the student is conscious, gently attempt to find out what happened, and the nature of the injury. If the screening process was thorough the coach should already be aware of any health problems that might have contributed to the incident. Such information should, of course, be made available to those administering first aid or treatment.

Accurate assessment of an injury and initial treatment speeds up the participant's recovery, rehabilitation and return to the sport.

3 How to deal with an unconscious athlete

By definition, an unconscious student is oblivious to his surroundings and will not usually respond to questioning. The coach must be aware of the vital signs to look for in an unconscious participant.

An unconscious state can be caused by many factors. There may be a loss of blood or damage to the brain due to an injury, lack of oxygen to the brain and vital tissues caused by a heart attack or stroke, or long-standing medical conditions such as epilepsy and diabetes.

'ABC' is a useful guide to initial assessment:

* Airway * Breathing * Circulation.

4 How to check for effective breathing

With an unconscious student, there may be a blockage to the airway. Check the airway for any obstructions, such as broken or false teeth, or vomit, and remove them. Lay the casualty on his back, with the head tilted back to prevent the tongue from falling backwards and blocking the airway. When it is safe to do so, the athlete should be placed in the recovery position.

To check on normal breathing, monitor the rise and fall of the chest and the gentle flow of warm air from the mouth by placing a head close to it. If the student stops breathing, be prepared to apply the appropriate method of artificial respiration.

5 How to check for a normal heartbeat

The unconscious person's heart must be checked to see if it is beating. This can be done by feeling the carotid pulse on the side of the neck. If there is no pulse, the use of external cardiac massage should be considered. However, remember that external cardiac massage can be injurious if not carried out correctly.

By ensuring continued respiration and heart beat, either naturally or artificially, the circulation of oxygen to vital tissues will take place and so the risk of further damage will be minimised.

6 How to deal with a conscious athlete

The conscious person is obviously easier to deal with, because he can give details about the nature of the injury and how it occurred. For the first aider or coach who has to assess the situation at the time of the incident, injuries can be placed into four broad categories:

1   no obvious sign of an injury, even though the athlete experiences extreme pain or discomfort
2   cuts, grazes and blood appearing in areas where it generally should not be
3   limbs that are twisted or misshapen, or joints that are at a different angle from normal; associated pain with a bone or joint
4   swelling, discolouration, lumps and bumps where they should not be.

7 Symptoms

The coach and first aider should be aware of symptoms associated with various types of internal and external injuries and those that might arise from the athlete's general medical condition. They should also be aware of the immediate treatment to give if necessary.

8 The control of external bleeding

Any external bleeding should, of course, be controlled and stopped. Even the loss of a relatively small amount of blood can produce surgical shock. With large wounds, pressure should be applied to staunch the flow. Tourniquets should *not* be used.

9 Identifying dislocations

Twisted, misshapen limbs and strange joint angles can be the result of an awkward landing or impact. Any such deformity could be a dislocation. Only a suitably qualified medical practitioner should treat dislocations.

10 Identifying fractures

Lumps, bumps and swelling can indicate the site of a fracture. Any casualty with head, neck, back, hip or leg injuries should not be moved if at all possible. If other fractures or injury giving rise to pain are suspected, again the casualty should not be moved. Bones sticking through the skin should be covered with a dressing.

UNIT 9
Training safety

It is the coach's responsibility to ensure that all participants train and compete in a safe environment. In order to ensure that everyone is protected from foreseeable hazards, the coach can do the following:

1 Screen all participants

It is essential that a new athlete is carefully screened to ensure that possible health problems are made known to the coaching personnel. Armed with this information and knowledge of the athlete's aspirations and expectations, the coach can work out a tailor-made training regime.

2 Take out insurance

Most governing bodies have insurance cover for their athletes, coaches and officials. However, it is essential that any required administration is carried out before participation.

3 Ensure a warm-up period prior to training and a cool-down period afterwards

It is good practice and a legal requirement that athletes are properly 'warmed up' before any period of physical activity. Such a regime should be systematic and progressive, and suited both to the individual and to the activity. At the end of a training session or competition, athletes must be 'cooled down' before resuming their normal life styles.

Any warm-up must be specific to the individual. An elite athlete's warm-up can be a training session for a less able participant

4 Constantly monitor students to make sure that they are not overstressed

The coach must be ever vigilant to ensure that no student is being worked or stressed beyond his capability or desire. Particular care must be taken with young and old participants, and with those with disabilities.

5 Teach only those techniques approved by the governing body

Most, if not all, governing bodies identify techniques of which they 'approve'. They also identify good practice in training and competition, and lay down guidelines and rules to ensure that it is followed. If coaches wish to introduce innovative practices, it would be prudent to discuss them with the appropriate experts.

6 In training and especially in competition or contact sports, match students for size and ability

Students should be paired or grouped according to physique and ability (with weight categories this is not a problem). The coach must avoid too great an inequality in size.

7 Ensure no overcrowding of the training area

Most sports lay down clear regulations about the dimension of playing areas and the number of participants per team. However, in the training area there are often few, if any, guidelines about the amount of space required by each student to train in. The coach must find out what the ratio of students to space should be for each type of training and activity.

8 Ensure that the training area is appropriate for the type of training being undertaken

It is good practice to train and compete in an area specifically designed for that purpose. The floor surface, training or competition facilities, equipment and lighting must meet the minimum standards set out by the governing body.

9 Have a knowledge of basic first aid

The coach must know where to obtain first aid treatment and equipment if he himself is not adequately prepared.

10 Be aware of the nearest hospital in case a serious injury needs to be treated

The assistant coach must have access to a telephone in case an emergency arises and the emergency services are needed. Similarly, when dealing with minor injuries, he must know the location of the nearest hospital casualty department that is open.

UNIT 10
—•—
The coach's responsibilities

1 The safety of the training environment

The Assistant Coach has a responsibility to provide participants with competent and safe instruction. Even though a coach may be designated an 'assistant', it is not an excuse for a lower standard of instruction or safety in the training or competitive environment.

2 The need for professional indemnity insurance cover

Most governing bodies arrange insurance for their coaches to cover them against claims made by students under their directions. However, just because a coach has professional indemnity does not mean that he should feel he can take risks with safety or relinquish his responsibility to ensure that all training is carried out in an acceptable manner.

3 The personal safety of each student

All students must be screened before being allowed to train or compete. An interview and the completion of an application form should ensure that the Assistant Coach is aware of their health, commitment and aspirations. If there is any doubt about a student's ability to undertake strenuous activity, he should be referred to a doctor.

The Assistant Coach must also be aware of regulations relating to clothing, footwear and jewellery.

A TYPICAL APPLICATION FORM

Name _____

Male/Female: Age _____ Date of Birth _____

Address _____

Telephone number _____

Give any details of previous and any current participation in physical activity _____

Do you suffer from any of the following?

Diabetes	Migraine
Epilepsy	Nervous Disorders
Haemophilia	Current/Previous Injury
Heart Disorders	Respiratory Disorders
Physical Disability	(Hay Fever, Asthma etc.)

Any other medical condition currently receiving medical treatment which may affect participation?

Are you currently taking prescribed or non-prescribed medication?

If the answer to any of the above questions is yes then please give details _____

Do you have the approval of your G.P. to participate in physical activity? Please give details _____

Are you aware of the physical demands of the activity? YES/NO.

Do you accept that participation in the activity might result in injury?   YES/NO.

Is there any other information which you think might affect or influence your participation?   YES/NO.

If yes, please give details _____

Signature _____ Date _____

Signature of parent or guardian if the applicant is under 18 years of age: _____ Date _____

The Governing Body reserves the right to decline your application without stating a reason.

There are many important personal and general health questions that need to be answered by new applicants. The coach can devise training regimes for an individual which make allowances for specific needs

4 Students should be made aware of the sport's physical demands

It is essential that before taking up a sport, prospective participants are told about the physical and mental demands to be made of them. It is a good idea to let them watch at least two lessons to appreciate what will be expected of them.

5 The need for parental consent for participants under the age of 18 years

Most governing bodies require that participants under the age of eighteen must have their parents' permission to take up the sport. Parents or guardians must first countersign an application. It's always sensible for these students and those under sixteen years of age to go along to two or more sessions with their parents to see what participation will involve.

6 The Assistant's responsibility to the Club Coach

The Assistant Coach is directly responsible to the lesson or session coach. The Club Coach must be fully satisfied that the Assistant Coach is competent to teach identified techniques and activities.

7 The class coach should operate under the caring eye of the Club Coach

The coach is not only responsible for the quality of instruction, but he must also accept the responsibility for students' safe training. He must be aware of potential dangers, such as the playing or training surfaces, equipment, lighting and the suitability of the premises.

8 Only techniques that are approved by the governing body and appropriate to the students' level of ability can be taught

To maintain standards it is obviously essential that the coach uses techniques and training practices approved by his sport's governing

Students should be thoroughly prepared for any period of intensive physical activity. It is essential that the coach ensures that no individual is being overstressed

body. Furthermore, techniques can be taught only when they are appropriate to the participants' level of competence.

9 A coach must use only that amount of force or technical ability that is appropriate to his students' level of competence

In contact and combat sports, coaches must adjust their expertise to that of the athletes'. They should not use their superior force or technical skill against a novice.

10 Accidents must be reported to the Club Coach immediately and any witnesses identified

The coach must report all accidents to the Club Coach and ensure that they are accurately recorded in the accident book. Witnesses must be identified and, where possible, the injured student should affirm in writing the accuracy of the report.

SENIOR
COACH
AWARD

Children learn through play. Where possible, training should be
geared towards 'fun'-type activities

UNIT 1
— • —
How to teach skills

1 The process of learning and the stages of development of skills

In the process of learning and refining skills, there seems to be a series of progressive developmental stages.

Stage one – the participant develops an understanding of the action and is able to produce a basic movement pattern.

Stage two – the participant is able to reproduce a crude but identifiable technique.

Stage three – by repeating the action under the supervision of the coach the athlete can correct errors and refine technique.

Stage four – with repeated practice of the technique the neuro-muscular systems adapt to the movement pattern. The action becomes automatic and stable.

Stage five – when a technique is repeated on a regular basis, the 'S' factors involved (speed, strength, stamina, suppleness and skill) will also adapt, producing not only a technically sound action, but one that is also effective.

With young participants, there is the additional process of maturation. Excellence in techniques requiring speed, strength, power and range of movement will be achieved only when those physiological characteristics have naturally developed.

Skills to be learned fall broadly into two categories:

closed skills – techniques performed by athletes as a response to a specific stimulus; a good example is the repetition of skills in class lines.

open skills – skills performed during a series of changing stimuli.

Closed and open skills can be exemplified by the situation in which athletes learn skills in class but then have to apply them in an assessment or competitive environment where there are many distractions, stresses and constantly changing situations in which the techniques have to be performed accurately, efficiently and effectively.

2 The learning curve

In the learning process there is an initial period of rapid improvement in the quality of technique as a result of effective practice. The rate of improvement gradually slows down until a plateau is reached. Repeated practice will eventually produce a further slight improvement before another plateau is reached. Progress is made in this step-like fashion.

3 The necessity for effective instruction

It is essential that technically correct movement patterns are learned and practised from the very start of training. This depends totally upon the ability of the coach to communicate visually, verbally or physically the essential elements of good technique.

4 The distribution of practice

The coach must identify how often a technique should be practised, how many times in each session it should be repeated, and, perhaps more importantly and often overlooked, how much rest is required. This will vary from athlete to athlete depending upon how best they learn, their levels of fitness, the complexity of the technique and the intensity of the workload.

5 Whole and part-whole learning

Should a technique be taught in one complete action or broken down into a series of segments that can be learned individually, then re-assembled into the whole movement? This will depend upon the complexity of the technique, and the athlete's skill, ability to learn new skills, level of fitness and, possibly, age and sex.

6 The effect of age on performance

Physiological development varies with age. In children there are critical changes around the time of puberty and towards maturity. Early skill acquisition should therefore be geared towards basic movement patterns involving body co-ordination and interaction with the environment. Specialisation should not take place until after puberty since motor co-ordination improves towards maturity. With the more mature participant it is the rate of learning, not the skill, that is the main factor.

7 Gender characteristics and performance

Physiological changes related to the post-puberty period identify the differences between the sexes; however, the rate of skill acquisition is not markedly affected. In western culture some activities involving females may be negatively influenced.

8 The retention of performance levels

Techniques that are 'overlearned' are retained better than those that are merely 'experienced'. The coach must accept that a certain amount of 'forgetting' wil occur in terms of the quality of performance from lesson to lesson. Participants will also develop skills better in a pleasant learning environment than in an unpleasant one.

9 The transfer of training

The development of specific techniques can be achieved only by practising specific skills. The practice of other skills might have a positive advantage to development, but not to a marked degree. So specific training will lead to the application of a skill in a highly specialised situation, whereas general training will provide many more options.

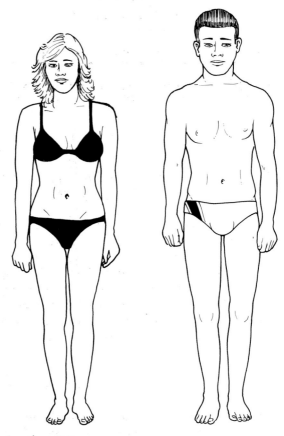

Gender and performance
Some activities, especially those which segregate males and females, might
require the coach's particular attention

10 Physiological adaptations to skill learning

This involves the physical modification of the neuromuscular processes assumed to take place whenever a change in performance not
due to growth or fatigue takes place. There is an actual physiological
change in the cerebral cortex. Ensure, therefore, that the correct
technique is taught right from the start.

UNIT 2

How to teach children and young participants

1 The necessity for training regimes appropriate to physically immature participants

Children are not miniature adults! They are both physically and mentally immature: their body systems are geared towards growth and learning. This means quite simply that training schedules designed for adults are inappropriate for juniors. Most sports were designed by mature men for mature men to enjoy. Young participants do not have the strength, speed, power, endurance or range of movement of an adult and so are not ideally suited to techniques that place demands on these physiological systems.

2 The structure of bone and the skeletal system

Due to their continuous growth, the children's bones are different from adults'. They are, in fact, initially composed of cartilage into which bone grows from 'centres of ossification' as the child develops.

3 The nature of bone growth

Growth in the long bones occurs by and large at each end in areas sometimes called 'growth plates'. These areas of bone growth gradually begin to fuse, which leads to the slowing down and finally complete halt of development. Their fusing occurs at different ages in girls and boys. In girls the shaft and epiphyses begin to fuse between the ages of fourteen and sixteen, and in boys between sixteen and eighteen. Absolute growth comes to a halt in the early twenties.

79

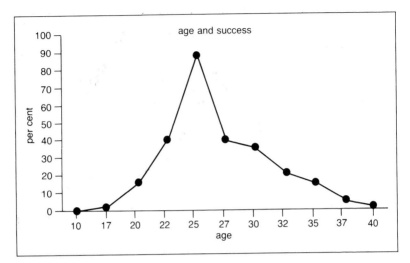

Age and success
Generally, sporting success and physical maturity coincide around
the age of 25

4 The rate of growth

The rate of growth in children is not constant; throughout the early
years there are 'growth spurts'. There are four identifiable periods of
increased growth between birth and adulthood. These occur earlier
in girls than in boys; therefore, girls are often taller and heavier than
boys of the same age. Once the epiphyses have fused, no further
increase in height can occur.

5 Endurance and muscle fibre type

The young athlete is better suited to an aerobic or endurance-type
activity than to short bursts of aerobic or intensive work. With the
mature adult, there are basically two types of skeletal muscle fibre:
   a slow twitch fibres are particularly well adapted to long-term
low-intensity work rates.
   b fast twitch fibres are especially well adapted to short-term
high-intensity work rates.

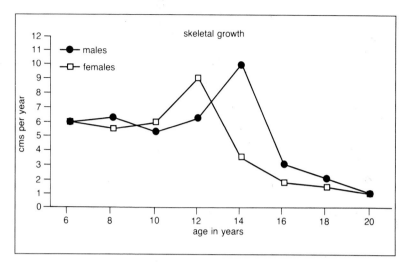

Growth
There are periods of peak growth which are different for males and females. Girls are in their 'growth spurt' between 10 to 12 years and boys, 12 to 14 years

However, before puberty there is no fibre differentiation, muscles being more suited to moderate periods of low intensity activity. The development, especially of the fast twitch fibres, comes only after this maturation period. As a result, children have reasonable sub-maximal endurance but they cannot sustain maximum training loads; neither can they produce explosive action.

6 The effect of hormonal changes during puberty

The hormonal activity in young people results in the development of sexual maturity known as 'puberty'. In girls this occurs between twelve and fourteen years and in boys between fourteen and sixteen years. With the onset of puberty the adult body shape begins to emerge as the last growth spurt takes place. Excessive physical activity during this period can delay the onset of puberty and the associated growth. Permanent restriction of growth can occur if there is damage to the growth areas.

7 The concentration span of juniors

Young athletes do not have the ability to concentrate on any one activity for long periods. An attention span of around three to four minutes seems to be the norm. To maintain both their attention and concentration the coach has constantly to reappraise his input to each lesson. Because of their lack of experience, young participants are dependent upon others, especially parents and their coach, for standards and ambitions. Because of their intellectual and emotional immaturity associated with the pre- and peri-pubertal periods, children do not handle failure and the associated stresses of training, grading and competition too well.

8 The effect of training on connective tissues

During growth the connective tissues are very fragile. It is easy to damage ligaments, tendons and bones, which can lead to permanent disability in adult life.

9 The role of participation in sport as part of a student's life style

All active children have interests outside the sporting environment that can give rise to injuries. Ensure at the start of any lesson that all participants are asked if they have any injuries, no matter what the cause. This is good practice with any group.

10 The 'play way'

Children learn through play. Where possible, all training should be turned into a game: 'fun' activities seem to be the most effective learning and teaching situation. There is quite a definite progression in the learning of skills which begins with basic body control activities and develops into the ability of the child to interact with the outside world.

UNIT 3
How to measure abilities

1 The importance of testing and measuring

Tests can be divided into two broad areas:
  a tests of 'Physical Work Capacity' (PWC)
  b tests of 'Motor Co-ordination'
It is important that procedures for testing are followed closely to ensure the validity of results and to allow for a comparison with previous scores or those of other individuals. The interpretation of the results must be left to the coach's discretion. He has to identify their relevance to the participants' overall performance.

2 The assessment of the contribution of the 'S' factors to technical competence

Most sports have a technical component. It might be the scoring of a goal or point that is the obvious mark of improvement in performance. However, how does a participant know if his technique is improving? Some sports have assessment procedures that identify developments in the quality of movement. When a participant achieves a particular level of excellence, it should be noted and identified. If possible, the degree of technical accuracy in the execution of that level of skill should be assessed – is it 50-60-70-80-90-100% accurate?
  Any physical activity is a discrete blend of:
- skill
- speed
- suppleness
- strength
- stamina.

The other contributing factors can be measured in an objective manner.

the 'S' factors

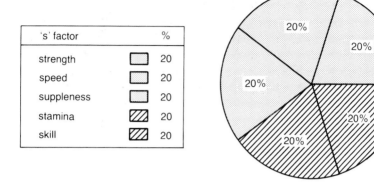

's' factor		%
strength		20
speed		20
suppleness		20
stamina		20
skill		20

The 'S' factors
The mix of the 'S' factors will be different for each sport and, in team games, for different positions

3 Measuring immediate speed (up to five seconds)

Tests – sergeant jump
– leaping decathlon
– throwing decathlon
– reaction time.

4 Measuring short-term speed (up to fifteen seconds)

Tests – four times ten metre/yard shuttle run
– tests requiring maximum number of repetitions in five, ten or fifteen seconds. Time how long it takes to repeat a skill a given number of times.

5 Measuring speed and strength endurance (up to sixty seconds)

Tests – the Comprehensive Power Test
– test requiring maximum number of repetitions in 20,

There are a multitude of tests of physical fitness such as 'jumping split squats'

25, 30, 35, 40, 45, 50, 55 or 60 seconds. Time how long it takes to repeat a skill a given number of times.

6 Measuring suppleness

Tests – lower back and hamstring flexibility
     – hip mobility
     – shoulder, trunk and hip flexibility.

7 Measuring strength

It is essential that the coach identifies the precise type of strength that is to be tested:
– isotonic
– isometric
– isokinetic
– plyometric.

8 Measuring medium-term endurance (up to five minutes)

Tests – three-minute step test
     – five-minute step test
     – selective work intensity test.

9 Measuring long-term endurance (up to fifteen minutes)

Test – 1½ mile (2400m) run.

10 Keeping records

It is vital that the coach maintains accurate records of the results of testing and measuring sessions. In that way he will be able to identify anomalies in the various components of performance that could have an effect on the execution of technique.

Step tests are an excellent measure of aerobic and anaerobic fitness

UNIT 4
—•—
How to improve performance

1 The identification and specificity of the 'S' factors to performance

Each sport, technique, sequence of movements and its application requires a specific and unique combination of neural and musculo-skeletal elements. These elements are usually referred to as the 'S' factors. Every physical action will demand a specific mix of these 'S' factors, the blend of which will be unique to that movement.

2 The development of specific speed

The coach must identify whether he is seeking maximum limb speed or whole-body speed, or the optimum that allows the maximum expression of force or skill application. Speed can only be developed by training at or above normal levels. Optimum adaptation to training can occur only with a rested neuro-muscular system.

3 The development of specific strength

The coach must identify the type of strength required: isotonic, isometric, isokinetic or plyometric. He must also identify one of absolute, relative or endurance-type strength as a critical factor.

4 The development of specific endurance

The specific nature of the type of endurance must be identified. The balance of aerobic and anaerobic workloads must be carefully assessed and developed.

5 The development of specific mobility

The coach must decide upon the degree of mobility that is required in a joint, or group of joints. He must be fully aware of the structural and physiological limitations to a range of movement. Regard must be taken of active, passive, yoga, and ballistic methods of training, together with more advanced concepts, such as PNF and stretch reflexes.

6 The creation of an effective learning environment

For effective acquisition of skill, note must be made of learning curves, distribution of practice, style of instruction, the 'model' and the 'grooving in' of techniques.

7 The development of the correct attitude towards the activity

To obtain optimum performance from a participant, the coach must behave like an amateur psychologist, identifying the athlete's aspirations, motivation, commitment, temperament, and mental preparation for intense physical activity.

8 The understanding of the demands of participation

The athlete must be prepared to 'suffer' for his sport. He must have the commitment and tenacity to persevere through discomfort, pain, periods of lack of success and boredom, and other training setbacks as part of the price of achievement.

9 The development of an environment in which participants can achieve success

The optimum learning environment is one that allows for a positive reward for effort. Every athlete, irrespective of ability and commitment, must have the opportunity to achieve success in every training session.

10 The development of an environment that will encourage students to continue to participate in the activity

A satisfied athlete will have a continuing involvement in the activity. It is essential that the caring coach creates a programme that allows each individual to achieve this.

UNIT 5
—•—
How to set targets and plan training

1 The need for realistic and accurate initial assessment

Before any training schedule can be designed the athlete's existing level of fitness must be identified. Areas of strengths and weaknesses must be noted, along with those that require special attention for a particular standard of performance, activity or technique. At regular intervals these levels, as well as the technical development of the individual, must be re-assessed to ensure that the student progresses in the anticipated fashion.

2 The accurate analysis of performance

The coach must be realistic with his appraisal of the potential of every participant. Similarly, every sportsman must be aware not only of his ability but also of his limitations. Any unreal ambitions will lead to a whole series of problems.

3 Systematic and progressive workloads

Any training programme must be based upon sound physiological and psychological principles if it is to be effective. The 'periodisation of training' is a programme requiring systematic and progressive increases in workloads, which allows for optimum physiological adaptation. These adaptive processes follow a specific order of emphasis in the training load. The coach must have a clear understanding of the physiological theory underpinning all schedule design.

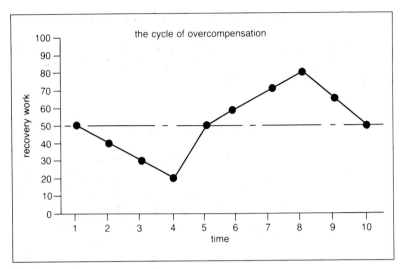

The theory of overcompensation
Any physiological system must be 'overloaded' to bring about improvements in performance. All adaptation takes place in the recovery period, which means that coaches must ensure adequate rest for their students

4 The basis of a sound programme

The first emphasis in the training load is that of general endurance. As it develops, it gives the student the ability to work productively over a long period of time. As the normal training session lasts between one and two hours, it is essential that the athlete can take full advantage both of the activities and of the technical expertise of the coach. The participant becomes fit to train. The workload needs to be aerobic in nature to allow for prolonged activity at low levels of intensity. The development of anaerobic work involving short periods of intensive activity can take place only after such preparation.

5 The development of general strength

The acquisition of general strength is essential for preparing the athlete both physically and psychologically for the more intensive anaerobic workloads that excellence of performance, and improvement in general, require.

6 The development of specific strength

Once a base level of both aerobic endurance and general strength has been developed, progressive and systematic improvement in technique needs to be worked on.

7 The development of speed

To avoid the risk of injury to joints and connective tissue, it is essential that those physiological systems involved in a technique or action are well prepared for maximal loadings. Because any speed work is predominantly anaerobic, it is logical that it should come at this point. Speed of movement is a refinement of technique, and as such it must come not only after a thorough preparation in general strength and endurance, but also when the essential technical requirements have been mastered.

8 The development of skill

Technical development can be achieved only with an efficient neuro-muscular system. Technical refinement develops in the same way as physiological adaptation.

- technically correct techniques should be taught and learned early on so that they become well established
- training should be balanced so that no one element is emphasised to the exclusion of others
- the importance of recovery cannot be stressed too much; it is the recovery period which allows the body to adapt fully to training
- the learning and teaching atmosphere has to be positive to allow for the student to develop at the best possible rate
- the amount of time available per day, week, month and year to train
- training loads should not be too intense too early
- general conditioning should have priority over any kind of intense specific training

---

The development of a sound training programme

9 Writing the programme

The design of any programme will be specific to the abilities of the individual and the demands of the particular sport. It must take into account other factors such as time available to train, finance, facilities and medical back up.

10 Student records

It is essential that a permanent, accurate and comprehensive record of training is kept by the participants, or by the coach. This can

Date	Time	Venue	Coach
Introductory activities			
Conditioning exercises			
Techniques learned			
Points to remember			
General comments			

A student's training record
Most participants in physical activity are keen to keep a personal record of their progress. When such a 'log' is compared with the coach's training programme, it can identify either progress or areas of concern

prove an invaluable guide to identifying programmes of work that seem more effective than others. It can offer a good insight in cases of over- and under-achievement.

UNIT 6

— • —

How to counsel students over training setbacks

1 The importance of accurate assessment

The coach must realistically and accurately assess the potential of the individual. He must also take into account other factors such as the student's aspirations, commitment and dedication. Realistic goals can be set only when the coach has a clear picture of the physical and psychological make-up of the student.

2 The analysis of performance

Every performance, whether good or bad, must be analysed by both the student and the coach in order to identify those factors responsible. The coach must be able to evaluate technical aspects, anatomical and physiological requirements, and psychological factors that, singly or together, modify performance.

3 The athlete's need to achieve success

It is not just human nature that demands success for effort made in sport. The learning process is improved if reward is an intrinsic element. A reward-for-effort system can create an excellent physical and psychological environment for both learning and teaching.

4 Motivation is the key to improvement

The level of success achieved by an individual is a combination of ability and the desire to achieve a standard of performance. Motivation may be internal in that it comes from within the sportsman, or it may be generated by others such as the coach, friends, relations, the crowd and so on – in which case it is external.

5 The need for commitment to the programme

There must be commitment from coach and student alike if the latter's potential is to be fully realised. The coach is responsible for communicating his technical knowledge, for devising and supervising training programmes and for becoming part of the student's life in order to find out what makes him tick. Conversely, students must give 101% effort, and unquestioningly follow the advice given by the person in whom they have put their trust.

6 Students must not be overstressed

Hans Selye put forward his theory of general adaptation to stress, which identified the fact that stress can be either physiological or psychological. Both are important to the development of abilities through improving technique and adopting the correct state of mind to improve performance. However, care must be taken to avoid overstressing the individual, or breakdown will occur.

7 Factors affecting performance

The coach must be sensitive to the technical, physical, emotional, psychological and sociological factors that an individual is exposed to, and the degree to which they are affecting performance.

8 Awareness of the athlete's life style

Without being invasive, the coach must have more than a passing interest in the life of his student for him to realise his potential fully.

9 The need for a balanced life style

The coach must understand the importance of an harmonious

balance between training and life in general. An over-emphasis on one will adversely affect the other.

10 The role of the coach

The coach must adopt different roles to suit given situations, for example: technical instructor, teacher, coach, disciplinarian, motivator, father figure, friend and confidant.

UNIT 7
Working with injured students

1 Understanding the recovery process

In order to understand the process of recovery, it is necessary to know the processes of healing. This occurs in four identifiable stages:

a   the absorption of damaged tissue, such as blood (bruising)
b   the 'gluing' together of the 'cleaned' tissues – this takes a minimum of four days
c   the hardening of the 'repair' to make it reasonably strong – this takes about three weeks
d   the reinforcement of the repair by fibrous tissue – this can take up to twelve weeks.

2 The need for effective first aid

Good first aid is essential to minimise the tissue damage and associated bruising. This will serve to speed up the healing process.

3 The need for medical treatment of injuries

Correct treatment of the injury is necessary for rapid rehabilitation.

4 The role of pain in the recovery process

Pain serves as a warning of tissue damage. During the period of rehabilitation, pain is a warning that the injured part is being overstressed.

5 The role of rest in the recovery process

If the injured parts keep moving relative to each other, healing will be slow and not very efficient. Therefore, rest is essential. All other uninjured parts of the body should be exercised as much as possible. As the healing process progresses, the injured part should be moved more and more, but only within the limits imposed by pain.

6 The maintenance of aerobic fitness

Maintaining aerobic fitness is nearly always possible by performing exercises that do not cause pain. Good aerobic capacity is paramount for any sportsman and, if lost, takes time to regain.

7 The maintenance of anaerobic fitness

It is often impossible to maintain anaerobic fitness. If, however, it can be done, it is a great advantage.

8 The maintenance of muscle tone

Muscle tone and strength can always be maintained by isometric exercises. The exception to this is the case of a specific muscle injury: the affected muscle will need to be rested.

9 The maintenance of flexibility

Maintaining flexibility and range of movement in unaffected joints is essential. This can be achieved by regular non-ballistic stretching exercises.

10 Reconditioning

After a period of rest, movement should be restored to injured joints. Affected joints will be stiff, and flexibility should be restored by frequent passive exercise. Any exercise should be repeated

Working with injured students
Medical advice must be sought by athletes and coaches. Both must resist the temptation to resume training before full recovery from injury

several times a day, but always within the limitations imposed by pain and discomfort. The reconditioning process to achieve a previous level of performance is fairly rapid compared with the lengthy time it took to achieve it in the first place. However, in the reconditioning programme it is always wise to err on the side of caution.

UNIT 8
A new club

1 The potential for a new club

When considering opening a new club, several important questions have to be asked, such as: is there a large enough population in the area or easy access for travelling? Are similar clubs already in the area? Would a new sport recruit members from other established activities? Will the use of a building or facilities produce prohibitively high charges to members? Are there best times and days for opening?

2 Identifying the requirements of membership

The cost, conditions, benefits and rules of membership must be made quite clear to prospective members.

3 Ordering equipment and stationery

Where an activity requires specialised equipment or clothing it might be in the interest of the club and its members to keep a stock of the common items. Obviously, such sales can boost club funds. Stationery and office equipment need to be ordered as required, or ready access obtained.

4 A successful opening

An official opening day gives a new club a great start. Advertise the event and invite local dignitaries as guests and to perform the opening ceremony. Such a gathering of VIPs attracts local media coverage and gives the new club instant impact, status and credibility.

5 Local promotion of the club

There are many avenues for promoting a club, all of which should be exploited. Local sports councils offer an information service for enquiries concerning sports and clubs. Local authorities display information in all public buildings and schools.

6 Using the local media

Regional and local 'free' papers are willing to print articles on clubs and individuals who have achieved success. Photographs add to the interest value of an article. Local radio and television are always looking for items of interest in the community.

7 Organising demonstrations

Organisers of galas, fêtes and sports days invariably like to include demonstrations of various sports and activities. Make sure, if you agree to put on a demonstration, that the club is mentioned on all of the promotional material for the event.

A well-organised event or fixture not only provides the opportunity for the participants to enjoy themselves and improve their performance, but it also reflects favourably on the club and officers involved

8 Local sports grant aid

There are many local organisations that offer financial assistance to sports clubs. Every effort should be made to identify these sources with the help of the local authority and Sports Council.

9 Servicing the needs of the local community

If it is to succeed, the club must serve the needs of the community and take an active part in supportive events.

10 Providing information for potential participants

Have a ready supply of brochures and club membership application forms. Identify an address and telephone number for further details and information.

UNIT 9
Managing the club

1 Organisation, administration and membership

Most clubs have a democratic organisation that allows members to be elected to specific duties within the club.

2 Membership and training fees

Any fees or charges for training must be clearly identified, whether nightly, weekly, monthly or annually. Keep accurate records and accounts of income and expenditure, income and other taxes might have to be paid.

3 Publicity

A portion of a club's income must be directed towards publicity to ensure a steady supply of members.

4 Organising classes

Decide whether to run classes for groups such as beginners, inter-mediates, advanced students or ones with special needs. Integrated classes have both good and bad points to be considered.

5 New members

Any new members must be fully briefed about the organisation, conditions, fees and other general information. New members should be introduced to others in the group and made to feel welcome. It is useful to run a 'buddy' system where an experienced member keeps an eye on a newcomer.

6 Competitions

Competitions and assessments are an integral part of most sports, but they need not be mandatory for all participants. Many individuals are quite happy just to participate for enjoyment and to improve their general well-being. For those who want to compete, ensure that all information is available and that transport and other organisational details are confirmed. Reports and photographs of individual successes should go to the local media.

7 Relations with other clubs

As the club is an integral part of the community, it should have positive relationships with all of the other clubs in the area. Joint training nights, competitions and social events will foster good relations.

8 Local sporting politics

It is vital that all clubs have a voice in the general organisation for sport in an area. Local sports councils actively seek representatives from all sports to discuss topics of common interest.

9 The qualification of coaches

One of the attractions of a club is the fact that it has fully qualified coaches offering efficient and safe coaching. Be prepared to subsidise club coaches to obtain or update their qualifications.

10 The club as an active part of the community

There is a need for clubs to go into schools, business, industry and homes to promote their activities. Similarly, there should be open days when the general public can go along and try the sport.

UNIT 10

Organising courses and events

1 The need for forward planning

Long before the event, write a checklist of 'things to do'. Confirm all bookings, conversations and any requests in writing and keep copies of correspondence. Ensure that organisation and administration are completed in good time. Leave nothing to the last minute; it does not reflect well on the club or the event organiser.

2 Identifying the financial costs

All costs must be identified well in advance and receipts obtained. Ensure that any fees charged for entry to the event more than cover the costs; a safety margin is essential to cover unforeseen problems. There may be sponsorship available from the local authority or sports council.

3 Selecting a suitable venue

Pick a venue that meets the needs of the event (e.g. that has adequate changing and spectator room). Provision of refreshments is both hospitable and financially advantageous.

4 Organising effective media coverage

Invite the local press, radio and television. If possible give them a press handout beforehand describing the nature of the event and any noted participants.

5 Inviting local and national celebrities and VIPs

Dignitaries are quite willing to attend a function, even if only for a short period. Try to involve them in giving prizes or awards. Creating good relations can be very useful to a club. VIPs can add status to an event and ensure media coverage.

6 Creating a club logo to use on all promotional material

Most members are proud to be associated with their club and want to wear clothing or use equipment that advertises their involvement. A club logo on T-shirts, tracksuits and jackets is an ideal way of doing this. The club logo can go on all promotional material and advertising, and on any tickets that are sold for an event or competition.

7 Producing a timetable

Prepare a programme that includes a clear timetable of events. Allow sufficient time for individual events, taking into account the possibility of items over-running.

8 Spectator, VIP, media and competitor care

It is good policy to have a separate area for VIP and media hospitality. Putting the two together can allow for dignitaries to comment on the event. Competitors should have adequate changing, refreshment and medical provision.

9 Event information

An announcer can be invaluable by giving information and results to both the competitors and spectators. Announcers should be able to see the area clearly and be prepared to be quiet at appropriate moments. Stewards can be used to give information and organise competitors, officials and spectators.

10 Presentations

The awarding of prizes is very important for the individual concerned and for the spectators. The award ceremony should have the pride of place that it deserves; it might be a once-in-a-lifetime event for an athlete. Use VIPs to make the presentation and ensure that there is adequate space for photographers.

ADVANCED
COACH
AWARD

UNIT 1 • *A coaching philosophy*

The level 1, 2 and 3 coaching awards are geared towards identifying the general elements of good practice in coaching, administration and organisation. The previous sections have looked at the general skills which the coach should develop to improve his coaching competence. However, by the time he has progressed to level 4 there is a need for sport-specific specialisation, though of course there will still be elements common to other sports.

At level 4 the coach should possess competence in the more technically and tactically demanding aspects of the sport. However, he might also be responsible for several clubs and be the head of a group or an association of several hundred members. Within such an association or a large governing body with many thousand members coaches might be required to have specific roles, such as:
- national squad coach – adult (males)
- national squad coach – adult (females)
- national squad coach – junior members (males and females)
- responsibility for technical development
- director of coach education
- responsibility for special needs groups.

It is quite clear that with sport-specific demands the specialist requirements of coaches will vary considerably. At level 4, although it is possible to identify the elements common to most activities, it is not possible to be too specific. The following sections identify the component units that might be included at this level of operation. As explained, they can only be general guidelines, since the nature and application of such knowledge will be sport-specific. The requirements of each sport or post of responsibility will influence their structure.

1 The historical development of the sport
2 The traditions of teaching the sport
3 The individuality of the coach's experience
4 The individuality of the coach's philosophy
5 The coach's personal involvement with the participants
6 The recognition and appreciation of coaching expertise
7 The development of coaching competence
8 Identifying participants' sets of values
9 The coach's responsibilities
10 The rewards of coaching

UNIT 2 • *The development of technical excellence*

1. Skill development and age
2. Theories of learning
3. The stages of skill development
4. Introducing new skills
5. Whole and part-whole learning
6. The learning drive
7. The distribution of practice
8. Observation and analysis
9. Feedback
10. Diagnosis and correction of faults

UNIT 3 • *The development of mobility*

1. The physiology of mobility
2. Structural limitations
3. Elasticity of muscle
4. Resistance of protagonist muscles
5. Tendons and ligaments
6. The stretch reflex
7. Types of mobility
8. The effect of temperature
9. The effect of gender characteristics
10. The effect of injury

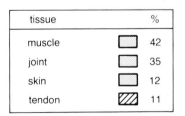

tissue		%
muscle	☐	42
joint	☐	35
skin	☐	12
tendon	▨	11

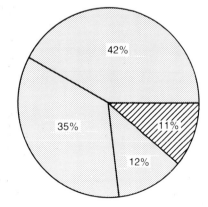

Structures limiting mobility
The connective tissues tend to be the main limiters of range of movement

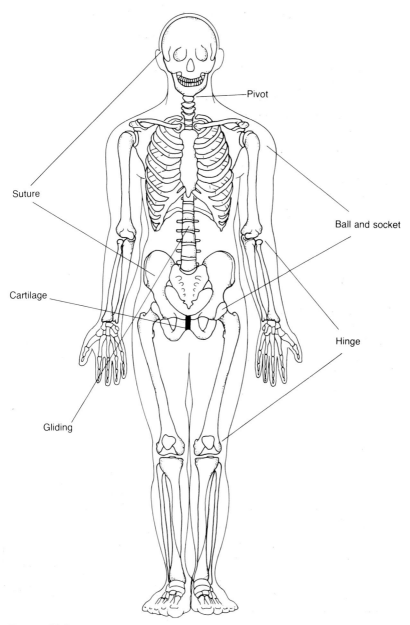

Pivot

Suture

Ball and socket

Cartilage

Hinge

Gliding

Types of joint
The coach should be aware of the structural limitations to movement of the
different types of joint

UNIT 4 • *The development of strength*

1 The physiology of muscular contraction
2 Isotonic muscle action
3 Isometric muscle action
4 Isokinetic muscle action
5 Plyometric muscle action
6 The principle of 'overload'
7 The effect of age and gender characteristics
8 Progressive resistance training

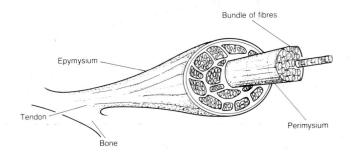

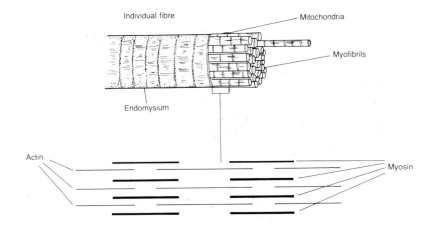

The structure of skeletal muscle
The coach should understand the mechanisms which control the speed and force of muscular contraction if he is to bring about specific adaptations in individual athletes

9   Strength development with equipment
10 Strength development without equipment

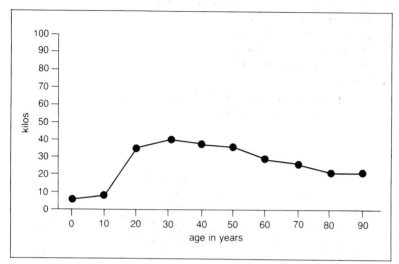

Age and strength
Strength peaks at approximately 30 years of age and then declines slowly
until 50 years

UNIT 5 • *The development of speed*

1   The physiology of movement at speed
2   The 'load velocity' curve
3   The speed–power–strength continuum
4   Short term energy production
5   The effect of range of movement
6   The effect of relaxation
7   The effect of muscle elasticity
8   Speed of reaction
9   The effect of age and gender characteristics
10 The development of speed

UNIT 6 • *The development of endurance*

1 The physiology of anaerobic endurance
2 The physiology of aerobic endurance
3 Speed endurance
4 Short term endurance
5 Medium term endurance
6 Long term endurance
7 Local muscular endurance
8 The effect of age and gender characteristics
9 The specificity of endurance
10 The development of endurance

UNIT 7 • *The biomechanical analysis of techniques*

1 The identification of forces
2 Units of measurement
3 Definition of terms
4 The identification of variable factors
5 Newton's laws of motion
6 Levers
7 Projectiles
8 Conservation of energy
9 Segmental analysis
10 Analysis of techniques

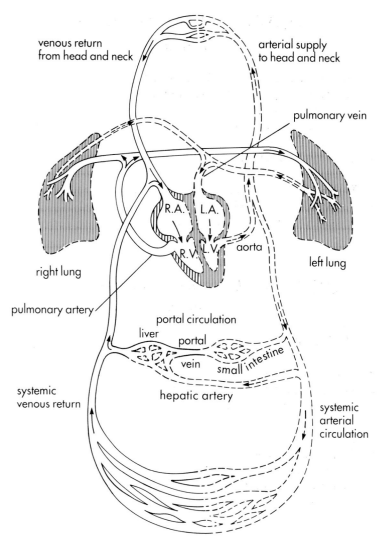

venous return from head and neck

arterial supply to head and neck

pulmonary vein

R.A. L.A.

R.V. L.V. aorta

right lung

left lung

pulmonary artery

portal circulation

liver portal

vein small intestine

systemic venous return

hepatic artery

systemic arterial circulation

Endurance

General endurance or stamina requires an understanding of the interaction of the lungs, heart, circulatory system and the nutrient and gas transport mechanisms

UNIT 8 • *Factors affecting performance*

1 Homeostasis
2 Circadian rhythms
3 Age up to twenty-five
4 Age from twenty-five
5 Gender
6 Life style
7 Temperature
8 Altitude
9 Ergogenic aids
10 Motivation and commitment

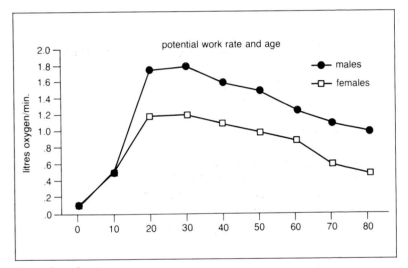

Age and work rate
There is a gradual decline in work rate with age. Peaking around 25 years of age, work rate declines gradually throughout life. Males tend to have a slightly higher work rate than females of the same age

UNIT 9 • *Nutrition*

1 Identification of categories of nutrients
2 Energy systems
3 Energy requirements
4 Factors affecting energy requirements
5 Special dietary regimes
6 Individual energy requirements
7 Weight loss
8 Weight gain
9 Planning a diet
10 Pre-event dietary procedure

UNIT 10 • *Planning the programme*

1 The specificity of training
2 The theory of 'overload'
3 Physiological adaptation
4 Progression
5 Reversibility
6 Testing and measurement
7 The 'general adaptation to stress' theory
8 Principles of the periodisation of training
9 Training or straining
10 Designing individual programmes

Assessment

— • —

The previous sections have set out the general education programme that a coach could experience in his particular sport. However, the simple fact that a potential coach has attended an appropriate governing body course will not automatically confer on him the status of 'coach'. Governing body coaching awards and their comparative NVQ will be awarded on the basis of the coach being assessed in his normal coaching environment. The governing bodies of sport will identify suitably qualified personnel to observe and assess coaches while they are coaching. These assessments will cover the coach's competence to carry out duties expected of him and which are appropriate to a particular level of coaching. Obviously, different sports will have varied requirements with respect to equipment, safety, organisation and administration. However, the essential elements of competent coaching will be common to all.

The principle method of assessment will be based on the assessors observing the coach carrying out his duties, although they may supplement their appraisal with specific questioning. They may also examine any written, visual or other material which supports the coach's abilities.

As previously discussed, there will be five levels of coaching. The first four levels are those appropriate to the practising coach. The fifth level is more of a sports science/sport administration qualification directed at management or those who will make an input into the national structure of the sport. Since they are not usually contributing at a 'grass roots level', it will be the responsibility of each governing body to identify the skills deemed appropriate for this level.

Within the four main coaching levels different activities will require additional sport-specific skills. For example some activities involve only adults and so the coach needs to be able to deal with mature athletes, whereas other sports recruit strongly among children, which requires a special understanding of youngsters' psychological and physiological needs to ensure that they are not being abused physically, emotionally or intellectually.

Another group of participants is becoming an important part of any sports membership and this is known euphemistically as 'special needs'. Such groups are made up of individuals with physiological or psychological conditions that restrict their potential to achieve. Their condition might relate to age; gender; sensory dysfunction, such as blindness or deafness; physical dysfunction, as in the case of amputees or paraplegics; mental dysfunction, as with Downes Syndrome or cerebral palsy. Any such disadvantage, while not preventing individuals from experiencing the full range of benefits to be derived from participation in a sport, will make extra demands on the coach to ensure their complete safety.

In summary: the four coaching levels have additional assessable coaching elements to ensure that a coach has the competence, necessary skills and knowledge to work with specific groups of athletes, adults, children and those with special needs. There will be a basic level of competence for any sport, usually that appropriate for adults. Once a coach has obtained a coaching qualification for this group he does not have to go through the whole education process again in order, for example, to coach children. He need only pick up the particular unit of knowledge that deals specifically with children. The same is true for coaching individuals with special needs.

The following sections identify the types of skills and competences that a coach should have to be effective, efficient and safe. Because there is a need for a commonality of good practice they are general and may miss out certain sports-specific requirements. The main reason for their generality is so that skills developed in coaching one activity can be transferred to other coaching or vocational awards.

Communication, organisation and administration skills are obviously the core elements to effective coaching. These are attributes common to good practice in all sports. Competence in any of these elements must be complemented by the coach's knowledge and understanding of his own sport's techniques. To obtain a coaching award assessment will basically fall into two areas. Governing bodies will be responsible for assessing the coach's sport-specific knowledge and understanding. To convert a governing body coaching award to an NVQ, those communication, organisation and administration skills common to all sports are then assessed. This

Analysing performance
The coach plays a vital role in giving the individual 'feedback' about his performance. There can arise a condition known as 'Paralysis by analysis' when too much or confusing feedback is given to an athlete. In such an instance performance is adversely affected

appraisal will be carried out by personnel from within the sport and by independent verifiers from other organisations who will ensure a commonality of standards.

For each level and specific group, there will be a checklist of competences. Assessors will observe the coach in the 'workplace' during several lessons and will 'tick off' a particular element when the coach carries out an appropriate task. Once all the elements have been verified, the coach will be awarded that level of coaching.

The coach as assessor

1 Recognising the individual qualities, potential and requirements of each participant

The coach should:

a   obtain basic information from the athlete: name, address, telephone number, age, gender, relevant medical history that may influence performance, and prior general and specific participation

b   identify the physiological, psychological, sociological, emotional, technical, and tactical aspirations of the athlete and assess how they might be achieved in the four levels of participation (foundation, preparation, performance and excellence)

2 Identifying the national structure of the sport and how it facilitates the organisation and functioning of the activity

The sport-specific structure consists of the international, national and regional governing bodies, local authorities, local clubs, and local facilities and their providers.

The general sporting structure consists of the national, regional and local sports councils, the British Coaching Foundation and sources of funding.

3 Evaluating the experience and ability of coaches

a   previous and current personal sporting experience, skills and knowledge

b   previous and current coaching experience

c relevant qualifications

d appropriate personality for the individual or group.

FOR ASSESSMENT PURPOSES the coach should be able to demonstrate an understanding of the implications for each athlete's programme of the physiological, psychological, emotional and sociological factors affecting performance. He should also be able to identify how such factors influence specific groups of athletes: children (growth and maturation being particularly relevant, veterans, the disabled, people with specific medical conditions, males, females, or any combination of the above).

He should understand the interaction of governing bodies, the sports council, national and local agencies involved in the development of sport at different levels, and know about subjective and objective assessment strategies, leadership and group dynamics, and the duties of the coach.

4 Making full use of the information obtained

The coach should use the above information to:

a identify possible marketing strategies to promote the opportunities for students to fulfil their potential and aspirations

b distribute to organisations, facility providers, current and potential athletes, coaches and support staff relevant details of training programmes, competitions, special events facilities and other related information.

FOR ASSESSMENT PURPOSES the coach should be able to demonstrate an understanding of implications for the programme of the implementation of marketing strategies and organisational and communication skills.

The coach as judge of the effectiveness of the programme

1 Evaluating the effect of the programme on athletes, associated personnel and organisations

The coach should:

a   assess the physical, psychological, social, emotional, personal, financial, time and commitment demands made on the individual by the programme; these should then be evaluated with respect to the age, gender and general and specific health and potential of the participants

b   note the demands of the programme on all individuals involved in its implementation: coaches, teachers, instructors, ancillary and administrative staff, and facility providers. These demands should then be evaluated with respect to the individual's own particular level of expertise, physical condition, and organisational and administrative skills

c   assess the contribution to the efficiency and effectiveness of the programme of the appropriate administrative and organisational bodies: governing bodies, regional associations, local authorities, national coaching organisations, sponsors, club committees, and facility providers and managers

d   identify the programme's demands on those administrative and organisational bodies, in terms of: philosophy, policy, administration, facilities, personnel and expertise.

FOR ASSESSMENT PURPOSES   the coach should be able to demonstrate an understanding and knowledge of implications for the effective running of the programme with respect to: specific physical, psychological and social demands; diet and nutrition; growth and maturation; life style and time management strategies; assessment of the needs of individuals; and assessment of the requirements of supportive organisations.

2 Explaining the demands of the programme to participants

The coach should:

a ensure that the physical, psychological, social, emotional, financial, and time demands of the programme are clearly explained to the participants in the four levels of participation

b where appropriate, explain and obtain agreement to the demands of the programme from parents or guardians, either verbally or written, as required

c identify and discuss the individual's specific needs (physical,

The coach must be aware of the training requirements of individuals or groups with special needs

psychological, sociological, emotional, technical and tactical) with the athlete, parents or guardians as required.

FOR ASSESSMENT PURPOSES   the coach should be able to demonstrate an understanding, and knowledge of implications for the sport with respect to individual physical and psychological needs, life style and time management strategies, communication and presentation techniques, and motivation strategies.

3 Explaining the demands of the programme to external agencies

External agencies should be appraised of:
a   the demands of the programme in terms of philosophy, policy, administration, finance, equipment, personnel and time
b   the implication of the programme in terms of planning, promotion, structure, facilitation, and implementation.

FOR ASSESSMENT PURPOSES   the coach should be able to demonstrate an understanding and knowledge of the implications of organisational and communication skills.

The coach as planner of the programme

1 Planning the programme

The coach should:

a   identify and evaluate the demands of the training load with respect to the following factors: frequency, duration, intensity and volume; and to the participants' current and required physical condition, specific conditioning programme, skill, tactics, current sporting status, degree of commitment, general interest, equipment; and other conditions

b   establish a timescale for achievement of activities with respect to priorities, deadlines, specific responsibilities and lines of communication

c   ensure that the content of the training programme is appropriate for the athlete's current level of performance

d   ensure that the demands of the training programme are made clear to all of the personnel involved: athlete, coach, administrative and ancillary staff, and facility providers and managers

e   ensure that the personnel involved in the training programme (including parents or guardians) agree to their commitment to the programme, either verbally or in writing.

FOR ASSESSMENT PURPOSES   the coach should be able to demonstrate an understanding and knowledge of implications to the programme of goal setting, planning the programme, subjective and objective assessment techniques, and communication, presentation and negotiation skills.

2 The coach should be able to explain the environmental demands and implications of the programme to participants and external agencies

The coach should:

a consult the appropriate external agencies with respect to political, social and economic factors, and questions of expertise, facilities and equipment that may influence the programme

b consult the participants to ensure maximum possible attendance on the programme

c explain and agree with the participants the timescale of the programme.

Assessing the programme
The coach must be able to assess objectively the performance of the individual and therefore the effectiveness of the training regime

FOR ASSESSMENT PURPOSES   the coach should be able to demonstrate an understanding and knowledge of the implications of organisation, negotiation and communication skills, and of time management and planning skills.

3 Communicating information to organisations and individuals

The coach should:
  a identify the necessary personnel (coaches, administrative and ancillary staff, and facility providers and managers)
  b produce and disseminate relevant information (in an agreed format), such as programme information, changes and timescale; information about training and courses; personnel involved, dates and finance
  c establish verbal and written systems of communication within the organisation.

FOR ASSESSMENT PURPOSES   the coach should be able to demonstrate an understanding and knowledge of the implications of organisation, administration, communication and presentation skills.

Maintaining current accepted practice

1 Being aware of and implementing current practice in the sport

The coach should:

a ensure that all sources of relevant information are identified and reviewed: governing bodies, national coaching organisations, and international, national and regional regulatory bodies

b identify all related sources of information: published guidelines, literature and regulations

c process and catalogue all relevant material in the appropriate manner.

FOR ASSESSMENT PURPOSES the coach should be able to demonstrate an understanding and knowledge of implications for the effective running of the programme of rules, codes of practice and guidelines as set down by the governing body; research techniques to access all related information; and organisation of all information acquired.

2 Identifying trends, developments and constraints within the sport

The coach should:

a identify any possible sources of expertise to provide input into the programme generally or specifically: international and national governing bodies, central and local government, national coaching organisations, insurance companies, equipment manufacturers, and sports science and sports medicine facilities

b identify the accessibility of any such sources of expertise

c identify any constraints on the effective use of expertise in running the programme with respect to time, socio- economic status, finance, personnel, facilities and/or equipment.

FOR ASSESSMENT PURPOSES   the coach should be able to demonstrate an understanding and knowledge of implications for the effective running of the programme of the expertise available to the sport; organisational and administrative support agencies; and communication skills.

3 Disseminating all relevant information with respect to current practice to personnel and organisations

The coach should:

a   ensure that information distribution systems (meetings, courses, lectures, seminars, news sheets, mail shots, telephone, fax and/or media promotions) are identified and established

b   ensure that all relevant material is distributed to the appropriate personnel

c   establish a programme for monitoring information distribution.

FOR ASSESSMENT PURPOSES   the coach should be able to demonstrate an understanding and knowledge of implications for the effective running of the programme of lines of communication, information distribution systems, and how to monitor them.

The coach as reviewer of external factors affecting performance

1 Identifying and reviewing environmental influences affecting participants and organisations

The coach should:

a identify and review all environmental factors affecting participants and organisations: transport, occupational, home, educational, health, social, cultural, economic, ethnic, religious and political

b consult the appropriate organisations (international or national governing body, the Sports Council, facility providers, sponsors and/or promoters) with respect to any such environmental factors.

FOR ASSESSMENT PURPOSES the coach should be able to demonstrate an understanding and knowledge of the implications for the effective running of the programme of the interaction of sport and society, the structure of organisations and agencies, and methods of communication.

2 Identifying and reviewing political influences affecting participants and organisations

The coach should:

a identify and review any political influences (international, national and local issues, or external or internal organisational issues) affecting an individual's participation

b consult appropriate organisations (international or national governing bodies, the Sports Council, local authorities, facility providers, sponsors and/or promoters) with respect to political influences affecting an individual's participation

c identify and review internal organisational political influences

d determine the impact on the participants and organisations at all levels.

FOR ASSESSMENT PURPOSES   the coach should be able to demonstrate an understanding and knowledge of the implications for the effective running of the programme of the interaction of sport and society, the structure of organisations and agencies, and methods of communication.

Designing the programme to allow each student to achieve his goals

1 Identifying and agreeing realistic goals with each participant

The coach should:

a carefully assess the ability of the participants with respect to each level of involvement

b identify the short-, medium- and long-term aspirations and expectations of the participants

c specify and agree the goals for the participants in the short-, medium- and long-term

d clearly explain the participants' goals to relevant personnel: coaches, teachers, instructors and/or support staff

e assess and review goals.

FOR ASSESSMENT PURPOSES   the coach should be able to demonstrate an understanding and knowledge of the implications for the effective running of the programme of methods of assessment, goal setting and planning strategies, motivation techniques, and negotiating techniques.

2 Determining the time available to achieve goals

The coach should:

a identify and present a schedule of competitive opportunities: exhibitions, displays, matches and competitions

b identify and present the frequency of practice and training activities with reference to the requirements of both the participants and the sport

c agree formal, written schedules of practice and training with participants

d explain and agree with the participants the necessary attitude and commitment with respect to their current status.

FOR ASSESSMENT PURPOSES   the coach should be able to demonstrate an understanding and knowledge of the implications for the effective running of the programme with respect to training programme design, the principles of training, methods of communication and motivation techniques.

3 Identifying and specifying the components of activities required for achieving the programme's aims

The coach should:

a identify and prioritise the components of activities necessary to achieve the aims of the programme

b refine components to ensure that they are appropriate to the physiological, psychological, tactical, technical, emotional and social needs and capabilities of the participants at their level of performance

STAGES OF TECHNICAL DEVELOPMENT

STAGE ONE   - **Have a go!**
Very much trial and error

STAGE TWO   - **Crude Reproduction**
A basic but identifiable movement emerges

STAGE THREE - **Refinement of Technique**
Errors are corrected and the movement refined

STAGE FOUR - **Establishment of Standard of Performance**
The movement pattern becomes 'grooved in'

STAGE FIVE   - **Physical Adaptation**
Continued practice brings about specific adaptation of the body systems involved

Stages of technical development
There are quite clear stages through which an individual passes when learning a skill. The coach must facilitate such development with creative learning environments

c ensure that the introduction of components is planned in a logical and progressive manner.

FOR ASSESSMENT PURPOSES   the coach should be able to demonstrate an understanding and knowledge of the implications for the effective running of the programme of analysing activities within a sport, planning an activity, and designing training programmes.

4 Identifying methods for delivering the programme

The coach should:
a identify and present methods of delivery appropriate to the needs and capabilities of the sport, participants, personnel and organisations involved
b identify and present coaching methods that are appropriate to the needs of the participants and to their level of performance
c identify and present coaching methods, e.g. questions and answers, participation, instruction and/or audio-visual appropriate to the facilities and equipment available
d identify and present potential constraints, e.g. time, socio-economic status, finance, personnel, facilities and equipment.

FOR ASSESSMENT PURPOSES   the coach should be able to demonstrate an understanding and knowledge of the implications of coaching styles and methodology; governing body rules, codes and guidelines; and assessment techniques.

5 Organisation of facilities and equipment

The coach should:
a organise indoor and outdoor facilities and equipment necessary to support the programme
b check that facilities and equipment are appropriate for the programme in terms of size, number and condition
c check that facilities and equipment are appropriate for the needs of participants at their level of performance
d identify and rectify shortfalls in facilities and equipment
e ensure that the construction and layout of apparatus conforms to current safety requirements as laid down by Parliament, or by the local authority or governing body.

FOR ASSESSMENT PURPOSES the coach should be able to demonstrate an understanding and knowledge of the implications for the effective running of the programme of technical aspects of the sport, methods of assessment, organisational techniques and safety legislation.

6 Planning activities

The coach should ensure that:
- **a** each activity has clear, precise objectives within the programme
- **b** activities are purposeful and enjoyable
- **c** each activity is appropriate to the physiological, psychological, technical, tactical, emotional and social needs and capabilities of the participants
- **d** each activity is appropriate to the facilities and equipment available
- **e** safety factors in each activity are determined
- **f** each activity involves all relevant participants
- **g** group sizes are appropriate to the nature of the activity
- **h** group sizes are appropriate to the needs and abilities of the participants at their level of participation
- **i** group sizes are appropriate to the facilities and equipment available
- **j** appropriate presentation and information materials are available for telling, asking and/or showing
- **k** provision is made for sufficient time to be allowed for individual and team feedback; by means of questions, answers and/or demonstration
- **l** procedures for dealing with conflict are established.

FOR ASSESSMENT PURPOSES the coach should be able to demonstrate an understanding and knowledge of the implications for the effective running of the programme of rules, codes and guidelines of the governing body; how to analyse activities within a sport; coaching methodology and style; growth and development of the individual; presentation techniques; safety legislation; safety requirements or organisations and governing bodies; how to give feedback and deal with conflict.

Identifying and planning the use of resources

— • —

1 Identifying and planning the use of support personnel

The coach should:

   a identify the personnel to support the programme: administrators, safety support workers, sport support workers, facility operations personnel, competition adjudicators, sports scientists and sports medicine staff

   b identify the shortfalls (in terms of numbers and expertise) of support personnel

   c establish strategies to obtain support personnel

   d plan and negotiate the use of support personnel

   e obtain the commitment of support personnel.

FOR ASSESSMENT PURPOSES the coach should be able to select, identify and plan the effective use of personnel; use negotiating techniques; and motivate personnel.

2 Planning the use of facilities and equipment

The coach should:

   a plan the use of facilities and equipment, with regard to dimensions, lighting, heating, accessibility, security and safety

   b make sure that facilities and equipment are checked, and deficiencies of type, size, weight, safety, and/or appropriateness are reported

   c establish strategies to overcome deficiencies

   d identify the minimum standards of clothing and personal equipment that are appropriate to the sport, training and the individual

   e identify potential suppliers of clothing and equipment for participants

Planning resources
Where facilities are lacking, the coach must be able to improvise with equipment and 'bodies' available

f brief participants and personnel on the minimum require-ments of clothing and personal equipment, and on potential suppliers

g clarify obligations regarding the provision of the appropriate facilities with the appropriate organisations.

FOR ASSESSMENT PURPOSES the coach should be able to demonstrate an understanding and knowledge of planning and organisational techniques; technical aspects specific to sport; safety factors and current legislation; potential suppliers of clothing and equipment; and communications techniques.

3 Identifying and planning the effective use of financial resources

The coach should:

a identify the financial resources, e.g. earned income, sponsor-ship or grants required to support the programme

b identify all available sources of finance: individuals, organisa-tions and/or businesses

140

c   establish strategies for obtaining financial resources, e.g. promotional activities, grants and sponsorship
d   identify constraints on financial resources
e   establish strategies to overcome financial deficiencies
f   produce working budgets
g   monitor expenditure.

FOR ASSESSMENT PURPOSES   the coach should be able to demonstrate
an understanding and knowledge of financial management and the
structure of organisations.

Planning the collection and use of data
— • —

1 Identifying the data necessary to implement the programme

The coach should:

a identify the types of data necessary to support the programme, e.g. relevant research, personnel, participation, financial, environmental, scientific, technical and sport-specific data

b identify the source of data necessary to support the programme, e.g. books, reports, medical histories and personnel information

c identify and consult administrative, marketing, sport-specific, sport development, sport science and sport medicine expertise in using specific data

d identify implementation, evaluation and/or marketing constraints in using specific data.

FOR ASSESSMENT PURPOSES   the coach should be able to demonstrate an understanding and knowledge of data-collection methods, how to identify and use expertise and methods of communication.

2 Planning the collection and use of data

The coach should:

a identify the appropriate method of collecting relevant data

b collect and record data in a clear, concise and accessible form

c explain to personnel the purpose for which data is required

d identify an appropriate method of analysis

e establish verbal or written procedures for the dissemination of data.

FOR ASSESSMENT PURPOSES   the coach should be able to demonstrate an understanding and knowledge of methods of collecting and organising data; presentation techniques; how to analyse data; and how to disseminate information.

Directing the programme

1 Arranging a venue for the programme

The coach should:

a ensure the availability of venue that is appropriate in terms of dimensions, heating, lighting, safety requirements, specific equipment and line markings

b carry out the correct booking procedures for the venue

c ensure access to the venue

d ensure that financial resources – petty cash, travellers cheques, cash floats, bank drafts, hotel vouchers and/or other financial resources – are available

e ensure that suitable transport and accommodation is available

f make contingency arrangements for foreseeble emergencies.

FOR ASSESSMENT PURPOSES   the coach should be able to demonstrate an understanding and knowledge of the sport's physical and technical requirements, booking procedures, planning and organisational methods, and financial management.

2 Organising the provision of resources to support the programme

The coach should:

a ensure the availability of equipment and resources to be used during the programme: clothing of sufficient quality and in sufficient supply, with the organisation logo and team logo

b ensure that equipment and resources used during the programme are checked and maintained in a safe condition, and take remedial action if necessary

c ensure that adequate financial resources are available

d ensure that contingency arrangements are made for foreseeable emergencies, such as accidents, breakages, bad weather,

unavailability of personnel, and lack of transport or accommodation
  e identify support staff required, such as assistant coaches, sports science or sports medicine support, and administrative or ancillary support
  f appoint the support staff required.

FOR ASSESSMENT PURPOSES   the coach should be able to demonstrate an understanding and knowledge of the technical requirements for the sport, financial management, and planning and organisational method.

3 Allocating activities to personnel

The coach should:
  a identify all activities within the capabilities of the personnel involved and relevant to the goals of the programme
  b ensure that activities are allocated to the appropriate personnel
  c clearly specify activities to personnel
  d allocate activities in a time frame sufficient to permit performance achievement: research, preparation, planning, guidance, interaction and feedback
  e make appropriate verbal and written records and references available to personnel
  f make available the necessary facilities to carry out the activities.

FOR ASSESSMENT PURPOSES   the coach should be able to demonstrate an understanding and knowledge of the technical requirements of the sport; how to manage personnel; planning and organisational method; and time management.

4 Briefing personnel

The coach should:
  a make aware to relevant personnel the briefing arrangements
  b ensure that the environment is appropriate for the briefing, i.e. it is adequately equipped and has minimum distraction
  c ensure written, audio and visual briefing materials and sport-specific equipment are available

d brief personnel on the extent and limitations of their responsibilities and authority

e brief personnel as to whom reference should be made for occurrences outside their responsibility and authority

f determine the style of coaching for each activity

g explain to personnel the expectations regarding attitudes to participants

h agree and set organisational and sport-specific goals and standards

i make available opportunities for constructive interaction between personnel.

FOR ASSESSMENT PURPOSES the coach should be able to demonstrate an understanding and knowledge of communication and presentation skills; management of personnel; group dynamics; coaching methodology; and how to set.goals.

5 Operating the programme within the planned budget

The coach should:

a continually monitor written and verbal budget information

b adjust the programme in response to financial constraints, e.g. time, personnel or resources

c take appropriate action to ensure that commitments are fulfilled according to financial or coaching priorities

d ensure that all budgets function effectively within the range of responsibility

e elicit, and take appropriate action on, verbal or written recommendations and suggestions for improving the cost effectiveness of the programme.

FOR ASSESSMENT PURPOSES the coach should be able to demonstrate an understanding and knowledge of how to monitor budget information; planning methods; and financial management.

6 Operating the programme within the established policies and parameters

The coach should:

a clearly identify all policies pertinent to the programme, for example those laid down by the international or national governing body, the local authority or club committees

b   communicate all policies pertinent to the programme to the relevant personnel

c   brief personnel on the implications of the policies for individual participants with regard to standards and performance, or application and effort

d   communicate and apply policies relating to standards within the programme by means of information, warnings, sanctions and/or other disciplinary methods.

FOR ASSESSMENT PURPOSES   the coach should be able to demonstrate an understanding and knowledge of international and national rules, codes and guidelines; governing body rules, codes and guidelines; local authorities' and club committees' policies; communication and presentation methods; and management of personnel.

Preparation for conducting a coaching activity

— • —

1 Preparing facilities and equipment for the activity

The coach should:

a   identify and note current standing practices for emergency procedures within the facility

b   notify local authorities or other facility providers when necessary to ensure that the facilities and equipment are available and maintained in a safe working order

c   issue and store equipment in the approved manner

d   ensure that first aid and emergency facilities, as well as general, technical and sport-specific equipment, are sufficient and suitable for the activity and the age, gender, size and ability of the participants

e   modify and condition equipment for different participant groups

f   set out the equipment in a safe manner appropriate to the activity

g   identify unsafe equipment

h   mark or remove unsafe equipment

i   notify coaches, support personnel and facility providers of unsafe equipment

j   instruct participants to keep away from unsafe facilities and equipment

k   ensure that safe conditions in terms of playing surface, weather and equipment prevail during the activity.

FOR ASSESSMENT PURPOSES   the coach should be able to demonstrate an understanding and knowledge of current standing practices for emergencies within the facility; lines of communication; safety procedures and guidelines relating to facilities and equipment appropriate to the sport; storage and issue of equipment; facilities and equipment necessary to conduct the sport; how to deal with unsafe equipment; and methods of communication.

147

2 Producing a programme for the activity

The coach should:
   a   identify the level of each participant's expertise appropriate to his level of performance
   b   break down the activity into appropriate components
   c   identify the skills and techniques required for each component
   d   identify the rules, codes and organisational requirements of the international and national governing body, the local authority and/or club committee
   e   identify the components requiring specific emphasis
   f   identify appropriate demonstration techniques, e.g. question and answer, participation, instruction, audio or visual
   g   produce an outline or detailed programme.

FOR ASSESSMENT PURPOSES   the coach should be able to demonstrate an understanding and knowledge of skills analysis and development; technical aspects of the sport; rules and codes; requirements of international and national governing bodies, and of local authorities and club committees; coaching methodology; mechanical principles; demonstration techniques; and programme planning.

3 Welcoming participants and personnel

The coach should:
   a   ensure that the session starts punctually
   b   ensure that his and the participants' appearance, dress and demeanour are appropriate for the sport and conditions
   c   welcome participants and any visiting coaches, teachers and instructors, or any sports development or sports science personnel
   d   introduce relevant personnel to participants
   e   allocate participants to relevant personnel
   f   encourage participants to interact where appropriate
   g   record participants' attendance on a register, check list or record cards.

FOR ASSESSMENT PURPOSES   the coach should be able to demonstrate an understanding and knowledge of methods of organisation; how to dress for a specific sport; and methods of communication.

4 Organising participants

The coach should:

a   act in response to participants' previous skills and knowledge of their level of performance

b   brief visiting personnel assisting with coaching about their responsibility

c   clearly explain to participants the objectives of the session

d   explain the rule, codes and organisational requirements – of the international and national governing body, local authority, club committee and facility providers – to the participants

e   allocate space and equipment, both sport- and participant-specific to participants

f   clearly explain relevant safety procedures, legislation and requirements to participants and personnel.

FOR ASSESSMENT PURPOSES   the coach should be able to demonstrate an understanding and knowledge of skills analysis; management of people; methods of communication; programme planning and organisation; rules, codes and organisational requirements; and safety procedures and guidelines.

The coach as conductor of a coaching activity

1 Preparing participants for the activity

The coach should:

a ensure that the warm up is enjoyable for the participants

b use the participants' previous experience and knowledge of warm-up appropriate to their level of performance

c identify the level of physical readiness of the participants, with regard to health, disability, age and special needs

d explain to the participants the reason and value of warm-up

e identify and respond to the physiological, psychological and technical warm-up needs of the participants

f ensure that introductory activities are appropriate to the following work

g ensure that participants warm up with care during the introductory activities

h make sure that sufficient time is allowed for the warm-up

i make sure that sufficient time is allowed for discussion with the participants as required

j prepare participants effectively for the sport, by means of a warm-up, team talk, and motivation of individuals and teams.

FOR ASSESSMENT PURPOSES   the coach should be able to demonstrate an understanding and knowledge of methods of motivation; programme planning; physiology and psychology of warm-up; development of mobility; presentation techniques; and time management.

The coach should be aware of the activity's training requirements and should be able to devise individual elements accordingly. Any training exercise must be appropriate to the needs and ability of the athlete concerned

2 Presenting skills and techniques within the activity

The coach should:

a   use the participants' previous experience and knowledge of the activity

b   make relevant points of emphasis before, during and after the presentation, by means of explanation, demonstration, question, answer and/or participation

c   ensure that the presentation is technically correct and appropriate to the level of the participants

d   give the participants the opportunity to ask questions

e   re-present activities needing further emphasis or attention

FOR ASSESSMENT PURPOSES   the coach should be able to demonstrate an understanding and knowledge of the acquisition of skill; presentation techniques; coaching methodology; mechanical principles; technical aspects specific to the sport; methods of communication; and time management.

3 Directing participants in the activity

The coach should:

  a motivate participants throughout the activity at their level of performance

  b use appropriate methods of communication

  c use rates of work and progress appropriate to the needs of the individual

Coaching the class

The coach should be able to organise and motivate the group to participate in the lesson to the best of their ability. Not all students react positively to certain styles of teaching

  d check the understanding of the participants by question and answer and by practising skills

  e encourage participants by feedback of their results individually, in groups and as teams

  f identify and introduce aspects of activities needing further attention

  g make modifications to the activity when necessary

h ensure that the activity progresses appropriately for the participants
i ensure that sufficient time is allowed for the activity.

FOR ASSESSMENT PURPOSES   the coach should be able to demonstrate an understanding and knowledge of how to motivate participants; methods of communication; the acquisition of skill; coaching methodology; physical and psychological factors affecting performance; and time management.

4 Identifying errors and offering solutions

The coach should:
a identify and prioritise faults in technique
b give individual and group feedback to participants in an appropriate manner
c identify and use techniques that contribute to more successful subsequent attempts
d monitor the progress of participants.

FOR ASSESSMENT PURPOSES   the coach should be able to demonstrate an understanding and knowledge of observation and analysis of techniques; mechanical principles; and record keeping.

5 Preparing participants to end the activity

The coach should:
a organise an enjoyable cool-down
b use previous experience and knowlege of the participants to give them appropriate activities for their level of performance
c explain to the participants the reasons for a cool-down
d identify and respond to the participants' physical and psychological needs during the activity
e allow sufficient time for the activity
f effectively cool down the participants
g explain practice routines for the following session
h allow the participants sufficient time for further discussion
i explain to the participants the time, location and content of future activities
j supervise the departure of the participants.

FOR ASSESSMENT PURPOSES   the coach should be able to demonstrate an understanding and knowledge of the physiology and psychology of cool-down; coaching methodology; methods of communication; time management; and organisational techniques.

6 Accessing emergency services and initiating remedial action

The coach should:

a apply the current practices laid down by national legislation, the local authority or governing body within the facility for emergency procedures

b ensure the safety of participants, personnel and bystanders and spectators

c take any necessary action to protect the victim from further injury

d identify the location of telephones and appropriate emergency numbers

e identify the location of appropriate first aid materials

f keep a written record of emergencies, signed and dated by the coach in charge of the session, containing information about names, circumstances, time, date, injuries sustained and action taken

g notify the next of kin where necessary as soon as possible and in an appropriate manner

h ensure that any necessary first aid is carried out by qualified personnel.

FOR ASSESSMENT PURPOSES   the coach should be able to demonstrate an understanding and knowledge of currrent practices for emergency procedures; organisational techniques; and methods of communication.

7 Contributing to the participant's post-injury rehabilitation

The coach should:

a identify and refer to any available records of injury and subsequent treatment, such as disclaimer forms, application forms, parental permission or medical certificates

154

b liaise with and seek advice from medical and associated support services

c establish, in accordance with specialist medical advice, a programme of activity that contributes to rehabilitation

d monitor and establish progress towards regaining fitness

e ensure that rehabilitation is conducted by qualified medical or sports medicine personnel.

FOR ASSESSMENT PURPOSES   the coach should be able to demonstrate an understanding and knowledge of the rehabilitation of injury; monitoring procedures; availability of sports medicine personnel; and methods of communication.

Communication with people and organisations

— • —

1 Providing advice and information

The coach should:

a use appropriate methods of verbal (by telephone or in person) or written communication to explain and supplement the programme

b present relevant information – costs, schedules, instructions, information, and technical or individual support – clearly and precisely

c present relevant information in a positive and encouraging manner

d check the receipt and understanding of information by the relevant recipients

instruction	teaching	training	coaching
predetermined commands; activity is usually drills	opportunity to develop skills in a variety of situations	development of élite performance	development and attainment of a student's potential

level of personal contact with students

low   medium   high   1:1 intense

1:15

1:25

1:30+

Communication skills
The way in which a 'coach' passes on to others his skills and knowledge depends to a certain extent on the size of the group

  e encourage comments and opinions from the recipients
  f identify and correct misunderstandings
  g create and maintain a supportive atmosphere to encourage motivation.

FOR ASSESSMENT PURPOSES   the coach should be able to demonstrate an understanding and knowledge of methods of communication; presentation techniques; and how to motivate people.

2 Providing feedback on performance

The coach should:
  a observe the sport-specific performance of an activity and general pattern of movement by the participants
  b analyse performance against agreed criteria appropriate to their level of performance
  c identify faults
  d prioritise the order in which faults should be rectified
  e provide the necessary technical and tactical information and advice to correct each fault

The coach must be able to organise training and subsequent competition for all ability groups

    f   check that information and advice is understood by the participants.

FOR ASSESSMENT PURPOSES   the coach should be able to demonstrate an understanding and knowledge of methods of observation and analysis; the acquisition of skill; and methods of communication.

3 Leading meetings and group discussions

The coach should:
    a   select times and venues of meetings to maximise attendance
    b   arrange that records of meetings (minutes or transcripts) are taken by himself or delegated personnel
    c   structure groups to allow maximum input from individuals
    d   clearly state the objectives of the meeting
    e   state the parameters in which discussions will take place
    f   provide a clear agenda in advance
    g   state the time available for discussion
    h   elicit a cross-section of viewpoints
    i   ensure that discussion is pertinent to the subject
    j   take appropriate and effective action to control the meeting
    k   instigate the resolution of conflict or further action as required.

FOR ASSESSMENT PURPOSES   the coach should be able to demonstrate an understanding and knowledge of planning and organisational techniques; management of people; group dynamics; methods of communication and presentation; and time management.

4 Contributing to group discussions

The coach should:
    a   summarise discussions, verbally or in writing, to include a variety of opinions presented
    b   indicate consensus viewpoints
    c   identify and specify options available to solve problems
    d   identify options having majority support
    e   clearly state action to be taken to implement solutions
    f   explain and agree, verbally or in writing, action programmes and timescales
    g   identify and agree any further remedial action.

FOR ASSESSMENT PURPOSES   the coach should be able to demonstrate an understanding and knowledge of presentation techniques, methods of communication and group dynamics.

Creating and maintaining relationships

— • —

1 Establishing the needs of personnel and organisations

The coach should:
  a establish the financial, organisational, personal, professional and ethical needs of personnel
  b establish the financial, organisational, cultural and ethical needs of the organisation
  c discuss specific needs with relevant personnel
  d initiate procedures to ensure that needs are satisfied
  e review as necessary the needs of relevant personnel and organisations.

FOR ASSESSMENT PURPOSES   the coach should be able to demonstrate an understanding and knowledge of needs analysis; management of people; methods of communication; and organisational techniques.

2 Establishing inter-relationships

The coach should:
  a establish verbal and written two-way communications with relevant participants
  b establish two-way communications with relevant organisations
  c establish two-way communication with relevant personnel.

FOR ASSESSMENT PURPOSES   the coach should be able to demonstrate an understanding and knowledge of methods of communication; and the development of inter-personal relationships.

3 Establishing ethical standards

The coach should:
a   establish and use ethical standards laid down by governing bodies or the local authority for the conduct of the programme
b   explain to all concerned the ethical standards set
c   initiate appropriate disciplinary action for breaches of ethical standards
d   inform the relevant personnel of any disciplinary action
e   inform the relevant organisations of any disciplinary action.

FOR ASSESSMENT PURPOSES   the coach should be able to demonstrate an understanding and knowledge of ethics in sport; codes of practice; conflict management; and methods of communication.

4 Functioning as part of a team

The coach should:
a   identify and encourage contributions from other team members
b   identify and agree the responsibilities of individuals within the team
c   elicit and consider the expectations of team members.

FOR ASSESSMENT PURPOSES   the coach should be able to demonstrate an understanding and knowledge of group dynamics; motivational techniques; and methods of communication.

5 Identifying when to refer participants elsewhere

The coach should:
a   establish the thresholds beyond which participants should be referred to other personnel, such as the governing body, local authority, management or club committee
b   specify the thresholds and relevant personnel
c   refer participants to relevant personnel when a performance threshold is reached
d   agree verbal or written methods of communicating feedback from other personnel.

Some activities tend to emphasise the individual's commitment!

FOR ASSESSMENT PURPOSES the coach should be able to demonstrate an understanding and knowledge of thresholds appropriate to the sport and activity; assessment techniques; and methods of communication.

6 Determining responsibilities and conducting evaluation

The coach should:
  a define and agree quantity and quality performance targets
  b explain performance targets to relevant personnel
  c define and agree responsibilities for all personnel
  d define and agree the criteria of evaluation
  e conduct the evaluation

f agree and produce an action plan, including corrective action and training needs.

FOR ASSESSMENT PURPOSES   the coach should be able to demonstrate an understanding and knowledge of evaluation and analytical techniques; goal setting; planning; and assessment strategies.

7 Ensuring the involvement and commitment to the programme

The coach should:

a ensure that participants and personnel have all relevant, current information about the programme

b ensure that the director of the programme, relevant personnel and participants communicate effectively

c explain to all relevant personnel and organisations their involvement in the programme

d make available verbal and written facilities for participants to register on the programme.

FOR ASSESSMENT PURPOSES   the coach should be able to demonstrate an understanding and knowledge of methods of communication and presentation; motivational strategies; and organisational techniques.

8 Establishing codes of conduct for the programme

The coach should:

a identify and use existing codes of conduct laid down by governing bodies, local authorities and club committees

b explain to relevant personnel and participants identified codes of conduct appropriate to the programme and level of performance

FOR ASSESSMENT PURPOSES   the coach should be able to demonstrate an understanding and knowledge of rules, codes and guidelines; ethics and sport; and methods of communication.

The coach as manager of personnel involved in the programme

1 Allocating specific activities to personnel

The coach should:
- **a** identify the previous sport-specific and general coaching experience and expertise of personnel
- **b** identify specific activities
- **c** prioritise activities within the programme
- **d** set and agree objectives with relevant personnel
- **e** delegate activities to personnel with flexibility to allow cross responsibility for coaching as a team and specialist coaching
- **f** establish cost effective monitoring and evaluation systems.

FOR ASSESSMENT PURPOSES   the coach should be able to demonstrate an understanding and knowledge of the management of personnel; goal-setting strategies; and methods of monitoring, evaluation and communication.

2 Co-ordinating and supervising personnel

The coach should:
- **a** evaluate and agree with relevant personnel timescales for monitoring and evaluation
- **b** regularly monitor activities allocated to personnel
- **c** agree targets with personnel in each area of responsibility: technical, physiological, numerical and financial
- **d** regularly check the understanding of the activities by personnel
- **e** regularly evaluate the progress or regression of personnel
- **f** ensure that any remedial action necessary is taken concerning issues arising from the evaluation process.

FOR ASSESSMENT PURPOSES the coach should be able to demonstrate an understanding and knowledge of methods of monitoring and methods of evaluation; time management; negotiation techniques; and methods of communication.

3 Identifying and minimising potential personal conflict

The coach should:
   a   create opportunities for sound co-operative relationships
   b   regularly appraise professional and working relationships
   c   implement cooperative planning and evaluation procedures
   d   identify potential inter-personal conflict among participants, personnel and external organisations
   e   remove potential for inter-personal conflict.

FOR ASSESSMENT PURPOSES the coach should be able to demonstrate an understanding and knowledge of management of people; methods of evaluation and appraisal; and methods of communication.

4 Providing feedback on performance

The coach should:
   a   identify and use methods of monitoring the performance of relevant personnel
   b   compare verbal and written monitoring outcomes and performance targets
   c   discuss the appraisal of performance with the personnel concerned
   d   discuss with the personnel concerned – verbally or in writing – future programmes for improvement

FOR ASSESSMENT PURPOSES the coach should be able to demonstrate an understanding and knowledge of monitoring techniques; methods of appraisal; management of people; development of personnel; and methods of communication.

5 Implementing disciplinary and grievance procedures

The coach should:

a identify and use clearly defined systems of disciplinary and grievance procedure, established by the governing body, local authority, management or club committees

b explain systems of disciplinary and grievance procedures to participants and relevant personnel.

FOR ASSESSMENT PURPOSES   the coach should be able to demonstrate an understanding and knowledge of disciplinary and grievance procedures; and methods of communication.

Evaluating the programme

1 Evaluating activity objectives

The coach should:

a   discuss and evaluate the extent to which participants were successful in completing the activity

b   evaluate the acquisition of specific skills and the ability to apply skills in practice and in the competitive situation

c   discuss and evaluate participants' performance, appropriate to their level of involvement, in key areas: technique, tactics, fitness, psychology, time, endurance, speed, strength and mobility

d   obtain the participants' verbal or written evaluation of the context of the activity

e   obtain the participants' evaluation of the relevance of the activity

f   identify shortfalls in achieving objectives, e.g. lack of technical skills or ability to apply them; lack of fitness; lack of sufficient motivation and inappropriate goals or targets

g   take remedial action to progress future activities.

FOR ASSESSMENT PURPOSES   the coach should be able to demonstrate an understanding and knowledge of methods of assessment and evaluation; technical aspects of the sport and activity; methods of communication; how to diagnose faults; and programme planning.

2 Evaluating facilities and equipment

The coach should:

a   evaluate the suitability of the facilities and equipment for achieving the tactical, technical, physiological, psychological, emotional and social objectives of the activity

167

b evaluate the safety of facilities and equipment
c make recommendations to relevant personnel about safety, modernisation, cost-effectiveness and marketing strategy
d take agreed remedial action in conjunction with management, administrators, external organisations and support staff.

FOR ASSESSMENT PURPOSES the coach should be able to demonstrate an understanding and knowledge of assessment and evaluation techniques; rules, codes and guidelines; the Health and Safety at Work Act; minimum standards for facilities and equipment; and methods of communication.

3 Evaluating the content and structure of the activity

The coach should:
a evaluate the technical, tactical physiological, psychological and social content of the activity
b evaluate the structure of the activity in terms of presentation and participation
c take any required remedial action to progress future activities.

FOR ASSESSMENT PURPOSES the coach should be able to demonstrate an understanding and knowledge of analysis and evaluation techniques; rules and codes; governing body and coaching organisation guidelines; and programme planning.

4 Identifying constraints affecting the activity

The coach should:
a identify internal financial, personal, physical, resource and organisational constraints
b identify external financial, personal, physical, resource and organisational constraints
c evaluate the ability to minimise constraints.

FOR ASSESSMENT PURPOSES the coach should be able to demonstrate an understanding and knowledge of technical aspects of the sport and activity; organisational techniques; and methods of communication.

All personnel must be able to meet the needs of the individual, whatever those might be

5 Identifying adjustments and making recommendations for future activities

The coach should:

a evaluate the whole activity, in terms of personnel, participants, finance, marketing, resources, facilities and support

b identify any necessary technical, tactical, psychological, physiological or social adjustments to key areas of the activity

c recommend any adjustments in key areas of the activity to the relevant personnel

d make any adjustments in future activities agreed with the sport governing body, local authority, club committee, sponsors or promoters.

FOR ASSESSMENT PURPOSES the coach should be able to demonstrate an understanding and knowledge of analysis and evaluation techniques; technical aspects of the sport and activity; rules, codes and guidelines; methods of communication and presentation; and how to prepare a programme.

Evaluating personnel and organisations involved in the programme

1 Evaluating the effectiveness of personnel

The coach should:

a   identify and establish criteria to be used and methods of evaluation, e.g. a job description, organisational guidelines or performance targets

b   explain to personnel the criteria and methods of evaluation, e.g. observation, discussion, written reports or course appraisal

c   train and brief relevant personnel conducting the evaluation

d   identify and evaluate constraints affecting personnel

e   provide regular feedback, verbally or in writing, to personnel being evaluated

f   initiate and encourage two way communication

g   keep accurate records of evaluations.

FOR ASSESSMENT PURPOSES   the coach should be able to demonstrate an understanding and knowledge of criteria necessary for evaluation; assessment and evaluation techniques; structure of the organisation; management of people; methods of communication; and record keeping.

2 Evaluating the contribution of organisations

The coach should:

a   identify and establish methods of evaluation and criteria to be used, e.g. finance, resources, personnel, facilities, publicity, information and expertise

b   identify and evaluate constraints affecting organisations, by means of documentation, ledgers and/or discussion

c   identify contributions made by organisations such as business, charities, sponsors, governing bodies, local authorities, the government and the Sports Council

d evaluate contributions against planned objectives
e identify and record achievements and shortfalls
f make recommendations to relevant personnel
g communicate achievements and shortfalls to organisations.

FOR ASSESSMENT PURPOSES   the coach should be able to demonstrate an understanding and knowledge of assessment and evaluation techniques; organisational structures; methods of communication; and record keeping.

3 Providing feedback to personnel and organisations

The coach should:
a identify and establish verbal and written systems for providing feedback
b identify and collate data necessary to support feedback, e.g. written plans and reports; visual evidence; recordings and testimonials
c give feedback in an agreed format
d keep accurate records.

FOR ASSESSMENT PURPOSES   the coach should be able to demonstrate an understanding and knowledge of data-collection procedures; appraisal techniques; and record keeping.

4 Agreeing further development with personnel

The coach should:
a identify abilities and shortcomings of relevant personnel
b review previous development plans
c identify opportunities for the development of personnel, such as training courses, on-the-job training and open learning
d agree and record development plans for personnel
e confirm development plans to relevant personnel such as management, administrators and staff training organisers.

FOR ASSESSMENT PURPOSES   the coach should be able to demonstrate an understanding and knowledge of appraisal strategies; goal-setting strategies; development of personnel; training opportunities; and methods of communication.

Further evaluation
— • —

1 Evaluating advance information

The coach should:
a identify and evaluate the technical, tactical, physiological, psychological, emotional and social needs and varying capabilities of participants in relation to the programme at their level of performance
b identify and evaluate the demands of the programme on the participants in terms of finance, resources and time
c identify and evaluate external, environmental, organisational, financial and political influences on the programme
d evaluate the accuracy of advance verbal, written and media information against the programme outcome.

FOR ASSESSMENT PURPOSES the coach should be able to demonstrate an understanding and knowledge of the range, needs and capabilities of the participants; the content of the programme; the physiological and psychological demands of the sport; assessment and evaluation techniques; organisations and agencies involved in the programme; and methods of communication.

2 Evaluating the effectiveness of programme planning

The coach should:
a evaluate the schedule and timescale of the programme
b evaluate the planned programme budget
c evaluate the number and competence of relevant personnel
d evaluate facilities and equipment
e evaluate the method and use of data collection with information on participants, the specific sport, finance, organisations and personnel

f identify and obtain further data required to improve the programme

g establish revised programme objectives.

FOR ASSESSMENT PURPOSES   the coach should be able to demonstrate an understanding and knowledge of the structure of a programme; assessment and evaluation techniques; time management; financial management; management of people; methods of data collection; and programme design.

3 Evaluating the extent to which objectives have been achieved within the programme

The coach should:

a collect and evaluate relevant information on activities within the programme, by means of verbal and written reports, personal observation and/or programme critiques

b identify and evaluate differences between actual and planned programmes

c identify and evaluate any reasons for differences

d evaluate methods of assessment of participants.

FOR ASSESSMENT PURPOSES   the coach should be able to demonstrate an understanding and knowledge of the structure of a programme; data collection techniques; analysis and evaluation techniques; and methods of communication.

4 Identifying operational constraints affecting the programme

The coach should:

a identify internal constraints, such as facilities, equipment, personnel, finance, time, support resources and expertise

b identify external constraints, such as finance, resources, organisations, politics, socio-economic factors, time and expertise

c compile plans for remedial action

d make verbal or written recommendations to relevant personnel in organisations

e take agreed remedial action.

FOR ASSESSMENT PURPOSES the coach should be able to demonstrate an understanding and knowledge of the structure of organisations; assessment and evaluation techniques; presentation techniques; management of people; financial management; and methods of communication.

5 Making adjustments to the programme and giving recommendations

The coach should:
a identify and specify modifications to the programme
b identify and specify resource implications and modifications, with reference to finance, facilities, equipment, time, marketing and support resources
c identify and specify future ways to improve the programme
d identify and specify modifications to the number and expertise of personnel
e make recommendations in an agreed verbal or written format to relevant personnel and organisations.

FOR ASSESSMENT PURPOSES the coach should be able to demonstrate an understanding and knowledge of the structure of a programme; programme planning techniques; financial management; assessment and evaluation techniques; management of people; methods of communication; and methods of presentation.

Index